A GUIDE TO
Inspiring Abstinence

D0711362

LAURA B. GALLIER

Choosing to Wait

A GUIDE TO
Inspiring Abstinence

DESTINY IMAGE₈ PUBLISHERS, INC.
P.O. Box 310, Shippensburg, PA 17257-0310

"Speaking to the Purposes of God for this Generation and for the Generations to Come."

This book and all other Destiny Image, Revival Press, Mercy Place, Fresh Bread, Destiny Image Fiction, and Treasure House books are available at Christian bookstores and distributors worldwide.

For a U.S. bookstore nearest you, call 1-800-722-6774.
For more information on foreign distributors, call 717-532-3040.
Reach us on the Internet: www.destinyimage.com.

ISBN 10: 0-7684-2740-1   ISBN 13: 978-0-7684-2740-0

For Worldwide Distribution, Printed in the U.S.A.

1 2 3 4 5 6 7 8 9 10 11 / 13 12 11 10 09

Dedication

To my grandmother, Bonnie Ruth Bolls (a.k.a. Nanny), the *real* writer in the family.

Acknowledgments

I would like to thank my husband, Patrick Gallier, for the many sacrifices he has made so that I can pursue writing.

I would also like to thank my mother, Linda McClendon, for her ongoing support with this endeavor.

In addition, I would like to thank Shaun and Laura Cuttill for rallying behind the vision of this book—what a blessing you two have been!

Finally, I will forever be grateful to Ronda Ranalli from Destiny Image Publishers; thank you for believing in me.

Endorsement

If I was looking for a friend to help me develop teaching moments with my child or teenager in the arena of godly sexual instruction, my search could end right here. *Choosing to Wait* includes development of godly themes where sex is concerned, actual teaching ideas, and a comprehensive approach, including what to teach and do if my child is already sexually active. Start here, and start where you are!

Dr. Arthur Cornett, Founder and Director
Family Camp Initiative, San Antonio, Texas

Contents

Introduction 13

FIRST STEP: PREPARATION

Chapter 1: FORCING
What's Wrong With Forcing Abstinence? 21

Chapter 2: WARNING
I've Warned My Child—Isn't That Enough? 33

Chapter 3: INSTILLING
Effective Abstinence Approach 47

Chapter 4: DELEGATION
Isn't it the Church's Responsibility? 57

Chapter 5: HOME LIFE
What Affects a Child's Sexuality? 69

Chapter 6: TIMING
    How Old for Sex Talk? 85

SECOND STEP: APPLICATION

Chapter 7: SACRED
    What's so Sacred About Sex? 99

Chapter 8: SIN
    Why Is Premarital Sex a Sin? 115

Chapter 9: VIRGINITY
    How to Convey the Value of Virginity 135

Chapter 10: FOREPLAY
    How Far Is Too Far? 151

Chapter 11: DATING
    What About Dating? 169

THIRD STEP: MOTIVATION

Chapter 12: OBJECTIONS
    Responding to Objections
    and Myths About Abstinence 201

Chapter 13: MARRIAGE
    Preparing a Child to Choose
    the Right Mate 215

Chapter 14: RENEWAL
    No Longer a Virgin? 231

Chapter 15: LONG-TERM SUCCESS
    Encouraging Abstinence Commitment 241

    Appendix 251

    Endnotes 259

Introduction

"Welcome to McQuick-Fix. May I take your order?"

"Yes, I'll have your *Keep My Kid Abstinent* value meal with a side of *Make My Teenager Listen To Me*. Please hold the *You Don't Know What You're Talking About, Mom*."

"OK, what would you like to drink with that?"

"Give me a super-sized cup of *I Need This To Sink In Before Prom*. Oh, and throw in one of those low-fat *My Child Values His Virginity* bars. Those are good!"

"Please drive through to the second window ma'am—we'll have your child's abstinence ready right away!"

I admit it. If there were such a thing as a McQuick-Fix drive through, I would be a frequent customer. I like the idea of resolving life's issues quickly, affordably, and if at all possible, effortlessly. But you and I both know that words like *quick, affordable,* and *effortless* hardly describe parenthood!

The reality is there is no quick-fix for instilling abstinence in our kids. Furthermore, the reason many approaches fail is because they focus solely on sex education and never take the "bigger picture" into account. You see, our children's life choices are direct reflections of their individual moral standards and belief systems. This is why it is a mistake to ignore our children's spiritual development while aiming to somehow modify their behavior.

In reality, a young person's decision to commit to premarital abstinence is a *byproduct*—an outward expression of an inward conviction. How do we cultivate such convictions in our kids? This book is devoted to equipping you with solid answers to this question and providing you with the practical tools needed for effective application.

And speaking of a young person's decision to commit to abstinence, it is ultimately our kids' decision! That's why the emphasis of this study *is* about *inspiring* abstinence in our children, versus merely enforcing it. We can (and should) implement boundaries, rules, and standards to safeguard our teens from sexual temptation, but there is one barrier that supersedes all parental prevention measures—*our kids' personal determination to remain abstinent until marriage.* Yes, parents, we can cultivate this determination! Furthermore, I can confidentially say that the principles in this book are just as applicable for parents whose children have already had a sexual relationship as it is for parents whose kids are still virgins.

This study is comprised of three stages: *preparation, application,* and *motivation,* all of which work together to bring us to our end goal of generating *inspiration* for abstinence in our kids. It's important to note that this book is not designed for readers to skip around to the few chapters that seem most interesting. While I do not consider this text nearly as complicated as algebra, it is like algebra in that each chapter builds on the one before. The concepts in this study are best understood when readers start right where you are now and progress through the rest of the chapters in sequence.

As previously mentioned, there are tools provided throughout this study to make the ideas in this book as applicable and useful as possible, and I encourage you to take advantage of them.

I have written a companion book for teens so that parents and kids can each benefit from having their own reading material. *Why Wait? The Naked Truth About Sex and Abstinence* is designed to be extremely enlightening and yet humorous and engaging for a young audience. I encourage you to visit www.InspiringAbstinence.com and order a copy for your teen. The material reinforces all that you will soon be discussing with your child.

QUESTIONS FOR THOUGHT

Everyone knows that participating in study groups tends to accelerate one's scholastic performance. Likewise, working through this book with a small group of parents is extremely beneficial for all who participate. At the end of each chapter, there are **Questions For Thought** designed to spark discussions and allow group members to ask questions, share observations, and learn from one another's conclusions. Group members can also benefit from much needed accountability and prayer. While the **Questions for Thought** can be used for self-reflection, I encourage you to go through the study, first and foremost, with your spouse and also with other parents committed to inspiring abstinence, if possible.

PARENT-CHILD DISCUSSION STARTERS

In the Application section of this book, I have included helpful **Parent-Child Discussion Starters** designed to get your child thinking and talking about various issues surrounding sex and abstinence. The suggested questions serve as spring boards that you can use to promote conversations with your child about sex that might otherwise be somewhat difficult to initiate. Also, they get your child talking and involved, versus just listening. Further instructions for utilizing these questions are provided in the Application section.

DISCUSSION ROADMAPS

I have also provided **Discussion Roadmaps** at the end of each chapter in the Application section. These can help guide you during conversations about sex with your child as you work through the **Parent-Child Discussion Starters** together. They provide a systematic way to ensure that your conversations stay on track and that you cover all the pertinent points regarding a particular topic. You will want to familiarize yourself with the content from each chapter in advance and then use the **Discussion Roadmaps** to bring specific concepts back to mind as you talk to your child.

COUNT THE COST

Statistics say most readers do not make it halfway through the books they begin reading, much less to the final page. I implore you to determine to be "above average" and to finish what you have now started. What potential hindrances do you foresee in regard to completing this book, and how can you compensate for those interruptions?

But don't begin until you count the cost… (Luke 14:28 NLT).

Also, who might you include in this study? Before moving on to the first chapter, you may want to send out a few emails or make a phone call or two and see if there are any other concerned parents who would like to pick up a copy of this book and go through this study with you. There are multitudes of heavy-hearted parents desperately seeking effective ways to instill abstinence in their children; perhaps your invitation will be a much-needed answer to someone's prayer.

In closing, I commend you for starting this journey! I pray the truths in this book bless your family as much as they have mine.

FIRST STEP:

Preparation

Preparation

+

Application

+

Motivation

=

Inspiration

IF YOU FAIL TO PLAN, YOU PLAN TO FAIL.

As a young girl, I loved the movie *The Karate Kid*. In the film, Daniel wants to learn Karate in order to defend himself from bullies, so he approaches the martial arts guru, Mr. Miyagi, who, after a series of events, agrees to train Daniel. The boy can hardly wait to get to Mr. Miyagi's house for his first lesson but is disappointed when Mr. Miyagi asks him to spend the day painting the backyard fence. Daniel assumes he is doing a favor in exchange for Mr. Miyagi's training, so he completes the job and comes back the next day, anxious to start learning Karate moves. "Scrub deck." The expressionless Mr. Miyagi hands Daniel scrub brushes. Again, Daniel does the chore, hoping that it will satisfy his trainer and that they can get started on his lessons.

After spending the following day waxing Mr. Miyagi's car, Daniel has had enough! He insists that Mr. Miyagi start his Karate lessons at once.

It's one of those goose bump moments when Daniel realizes that Mr. Miyagi has actually been training him all along! The repeated motions of painting the fence, scrubbing the deck, and waxing the car ingeniously translate into effective Karate moves. (*Karate Kid* fans everywhere distinctly remember the ultra intimidating "wax on, wax off," technique.) When Mr. Miyagi challenges Daniel to a mock fight, Daniel is astonished that he is well equipped to defend himself.

You aren't reading this book to reminisce about the plot of old movies, but you *are* on a quest to inspire premarital abstinence in your child. The Preparation section of this book touches on a variety of issues, some of which may have you feeling a bit like "Daniel-san"—*when are we going to focus on the issue at hand?* Rest assured, we are laying an all-important foundation for the Application phase that follows. I am confident that, as you progress through the book, you will see how *all* of the material in each chapter works together to effectively train and equip you for the task at hand.

And with that, parents, let's silence our cell phones, roll up our sleeves, and take a look at the important question posed in the first chapter, *"What's wrong with forcing abstinence?"*

FORCING

What's Wrong With Forcing Abstinence?

This was definitely our least favorite aspect of youth ministry. My husband and I sat across from two sulking parents staring straight at us like we were the source of their misery. Now that the four of us were alone behind closed doors, they passionately pleaded their case. Unfortunately, it was a testimony we'd heard before from other distraught parents.

"How could this happen?" Martha Jones could hardly finish her anxious sentence when her husband interrupted. "Our daughter knew better!" Martha jumped right back in, "We told Emily over and over again *not* to do this!"

We already knew what a good student and sweet young lady Emily was, but her dad felt the need to remind us. "She makes straight A's. She's on the volleyball team. She's a member of student council. She goes to church every week, for cryin' out loud!" My response would have gone over like a lead balloon, so I kept it to myself: *Good kids get tempted too, Mr. Jones.*

The truth was, my heart was breaking for these two loving parents. They never would have guessed that their 16-year-old daughter was sexually active, much less five weeks pregnant. I'm not sure who felt more guilty, Emily or her parents. I do know that they were on a desperate hunt to assign blame to anyone and everyone they could. My husband and I were easy targets. "Why aren't you teaching our kids to have better values than this? We're appalled!"

We didn't defend against their accusations, and it definitely was not the time to discuss where they might have gone wrong as parents. They were hurting. We were hurting. But Emily hurt the most. We needed to focus on picking up the pieces and preparing for the future, however uncertain it was.

My biggest regret? I hadn't found a way to teach Tom and Martha Jones what I knew to be true about inspiring abstinence in their precious Emily. It was obvious that they had done their absolute best as parents to protect their daughter from her current circumstances. Unfortunately, it became equally evident, the more they spoke that day, that they had not been enforcing abstinence in an effective way. It saddened me to think that these adoring parents had no idea that there was a better approach.

During the agonizing moments of that meeting, I prayed that I would somehow have the opportunity to help other parents learn the truth about instilling abstinence *before* they faced this sort of crisis. Years later, my desire has come to fruition; the book you're now holding is the answer to my prayer.

Each year, one in ten girls under the ages of 20—one million per year—becomes pregnant; 40 percent of these pregnancies will end in abortion.[1]

THE PLIGHT OF EVERY CONCERNED PARENT

Protecting children starts off relatively easy. "Don't touch the stove." "Stay out of the street." "Never play with daddy's razor." As the years pass, however, things get much more complicated, especially when our children morph into aliens (a process also known as *puberty*).

It seemed like it was overnight that my daughter went from pleading for more Skittles to begging to wear skin-tight jeans. It can be a defining moment of sorts when you realize your baby girl is blossoming into a beautiful young woman, or your son's once squeaky voice is now deep and manly. And just when exactly did they decide that the opposite sex no longer has "cooties"? Life was easier when our daughters thought that boys were stinky and our sons were convinced that girls were no fun.

Some parents think it's cute when their child comes home from school with a crush. Others get sweaty palms and shortness of breath! Perhaps one parent remembers the innocence of his own childhood and easily accepts his child's newfound attractions, while another parent is haunted by the sexual deviance of his youth and fears the same fate for his son or daughter. The reality is our children should never be made to feel guilty about their natural desires. At the same time, we should not be naive about the pressures and temptations those emotions bring.

These statistics about America's youth will either shock you or confirm your preexisting concerns. Based on a national research and analysis report published in 2005 by the Henry J. Kaiser Family Foundation:[2]

- ☆ Nearly half of all high school students (9th through 12th grade) are sexually active.

- ☆ Approximately one-third of young women get pregnant before age 20.

☆ Around 10 percent of girls and boys have sex before turning 14.

☆ Eighteen percent of high school boys and 11 percent of high school girls have had four or more sexual partners by the time they graduate.

☆ Approximately one in four sexually active teens contracts an STD (sexually transmitted disease) every year.

☆ An estimated half of all new HIV infections occur in people under the age of 25.

☆ Nearly one in four high school students claim they feel pressured to have sex.

☆ One in four teens report that they "did something sexually they did not really want to do" as a result of feeling pressured.

☆ One in ten high school students reveal they have been forced to have sex against their will at some point.

FORCED ABSTINENCE

Those statistics can make a parent panic! I hate the idea of my children feeling pressured to have sex, and I can hardly bring myself to think about the possibility of my son or daughter pressuring someone else's kid! But what can we do about it? For many of us, the obvious solution is to set stringent boundaries for our children. If the opposite sex can't get to them, they can't have sex with them! Sounds reasonable enough—we'll rule with an iron fist and *make* our teenagers stay abstinent.

There's just one little problem with this philosophy that can equate to huge disappointments later. *We really can't **make** our children abstain from sex.* Oh sure, we can attempt to monitor their every move and watch them like a hawk, but if they are truly determined to have sex, can we really guarantee they won't find a way?

Think back to your own childhood. Did you ever manage to get around your parents' boundaries, discover a convenient loophole in the system? I was raised by a single mom, and she did a good job laying down rules. As a young girl, I wasn't allowed to have boys in the house. So my friends and I just waited until my mom was asleep and then welcomed them right through the back door into my living room. We asked the guys to leave about ten minutes before my mom's alarm clock went off. A gutsy move, I know.

I bet you're thinking, "My child would never do that!" My mom thought the same thing. That's why it worked so well! Even if your kid really *wouldn't* do that, could a certain peer influence persuade him into doing other things that go against your rules and his better judgment?

The point I'm making is this: *if our only tactic for keeping our kids sexually abstinent is to make sure they never have the opportunity, we are underestimating our children's ability to find a way around our boundaries.*

KIDS GONE WILD

Haven't you heard the horror stories of the "saintly" kids in high school who go off to college, only to get into loads of mischief and party their way right into academic probation, or worse, become pregnancy drop-outs? I've heard many parents comment, "How could she have been such an angel at home and turn into a crazed wild child when she left?"

The truth is, you and I have a certain number of years to enforce structure and rules on our children, and then they are no longer under our supervision. If our watchful eye is the primary factor preventing them from having sex, their abstinence will only last as long as they live with us (or until they discover a great hiding spot). Furthermore, unless our kids ultimately agree with our standards and embrace boundaries as a result of their *own free-will decision,* it is just a matter of time until they find a creative way to usurp our rules.

Eighty-eight percent of children raised in evangelical homes leave church at the age of 18 never to return.[3]

There is an answer for those of us asking, "Why did my child drastically lower his morals after leaving home?" It's not necessarily fun to hear, but the truth is, *our kids' morals were apparently only as concrete as our consequences.* When the fear of our discipline was no longer an issue, neither were our moral standards.

Remember, we're raising our kids to live independently from us for the large majority of their lives. It's not their performance at home that ultimately matters; it's what they take with them when they leave home that really counts.

Am I saying we should not bother with structure, rules, or boundaries? No! There are definitely guidelines for establishing constructive boundaries to help safeguard kids against sexual activity. What I *am* saying is that *there has to be more to our abstinence approach than boundaries.* If you're wondering what *more* we can do, rest assured, that's what this book is all about.

FREEWILL: A BEAUTY AND A BEAST

Doesn't it just melt your heart when your little one unexpectedly plants a hug or a kiss on you? Perhaps it downright blows your mind when your teenager initiates affection, but the point is, it feels really good when our kids express love simply because *they want to.* Unfortunately the beauty of our child's free will can become a beast when it's turned against our wishes, when they use it to oppose us.

You may be surprised to hear that your child's power of choice is actually an *asset* when it comes to abstinence. Nothing causes your kid's ears to perk up as much as when he or she hears you say, "The choice is yours."

We do our children no favors by adopting a philosophy that welcomes them to go out and have sex if they want to! But let's not run into the other ditch either, where we deceive ourselves into thinking we actually have the ability to make our kids' decisions for them. *As parents, we have the power to **enforce** abstinence, but very little power to **force** it. Do you see the difference?*

It's one thing to implement structured boundaries that help *guide* our kids. It's another thing to parent with a controlling spirit that seeks to *drive* our kids. *As parents, we make up the rules of the road, but our children ultimately hold the steering wheel in their life decisions.*

> If parents are too restrictive and controlling, that correlates with [their children's] depression and other disorders, possibly resulting in adolescents who habitually deceive their parents. Parental monitoring may be harmful when, instead of indicating a warm connection with the adolescent, it derives from harsh suspicion.[4]

When it comes to sex, we can threaten our kids. "So help me, you're gonna be a virgin until the day you're married!" Or we can motivate them. "Your virginity is yours to protect. Only *you* have the power to save it as a special gift for your spouse,"—same end-goal, two totally different approaches.

Children with controlling parents look for the first opportunity to prove Mom and Dad wrong. They will be inclined to have sex just to make the point that we can't stop them. That's a terrible motive for having sex, isn't it?

> When polled, 49 percent of teens said their parents influenced their decisions about sex most strongly.[5]

Controlling parents may appear unloving, but in reality, it is usually their love for their sons or daughters that compels them.

They are so afraid of something bad happening to their children that they compensate with unreasonable domination.

Freedom from controlling parenting is found when we read *and believe* Scriptures like Proverbs 22:6, which tells you to teach your children to choose the right path so that, when they are older, they will remain upon it. You see, we're to teach our children to choose the right path, not to overbearingly choose it for them.

THE OTHER END OF THE SPECTRUM

On one hand, we have the parent who seeks to force abstinence. On the other hand, we have the parent who concludes, "Who am I to tell my child not to have sex? He's going to do what he wants to anyway." This parent is failing to provide leadership through clearly stated expectations. We have a parental responsibility to teach our kids the truth about sex. In short, *we should set the standard **for** our kids, and then get busy cultivating standards **in** our kids.*

> **When [parental] monitoring is part of a warm, supportive [parent/child] relationship, the child is likely to become a confident, well-educated adult, avoiding drug use and risky sex.**[6]

As parents, we cannot afford to be dictators or spectators. Perhaps an accurate word picture for effective, balanced parenting is that of a coach. We train, educate, discipline, and encourage so that, when our kids step onto the field of life, leaving us to watch patiently from the sidelines, we know we've imparted the spiritual insight and maturity they need to succeed.

Effective parenting requires work on our part, and as you will see in the following testimony, there was a time when I struggled to embrace this mandate.

THE BOOK THAT MADE ME ANGRY...AT FIRST

I was so excited when I bought Dr. John Townsend's book, *Boundaries With Teens*.[7] I couldn't wait for this prolific author and Christian psychologist to tell me how to change my children's bad behavior and irritating issues. I must say, I was quite disappointed after reading a few chapters—not because the book was lacking in content, but because the content showed me where I was lacking as a parent. I kept looking for "Ten Easy Steps to Transform Your Child," but instead I found one principle after another that challenged *me* to grow, change, and improve my parenting techniques. I'm ashamed to admit it, but I almost quit reading the book because I was not emotionally prepared to focus on me. Quite honestly, it made me angry! I bought the book so I could fix my kids, but the author kept exposing *my* lack of patience, *my* need for more compassion, and *my* responsibility to pursue greater spiritual sensitivity. It was a bit overwhelming.

On further consideration, however, I could not deny that what he was saying was true. I was forced to face the fact that the majority of my kids' issues were a direct result of my issues as a parent. It stung at first, but I soon saw it as a wonderful opportunity. You see, I cannot make others change, but I *do* have the ability to initiate change in my own life. I don't have to wait on anyone else. I can simply make up my mind that, by God's grace, I'm going to do things differently today than I did yesterday.

Perhaps you picked up this book about inspiring abstinence in your child and thought the same thing I did when I bought *Boundaries With Teens—this book is going to tell me how to fix my children*. While we will often look at issues surrounding your child's decisions and behavior, I must warn you, each chapter in this study is going to present opportunities for you to grow and change. Only when you have accepted personal responsibility for your part in inspiring abstinence in your child will you see the principles in this book take shape in his or her life.

Ninety-one percent of teens ages 15 to 17 that have not had sex said they were influenced by what their parents taught them about sex.[8]

I believe you are reading this book because you are serious about instilling sexual purity in your child. In order to honor that desire in you, I must tell you the truth. And the truth of the matter is that our children's choices and behavior are largely the end result of what we have put into them (or failed to put into them in many cases). Certainly, they have a free will and are born with unique personality traits and desires, but their character is most influenced by what we do or don't teach them at home. I want to see you become equipped to teach your child spiritual truths with confidence, which may require some major adjustments on your part. The important thing is that you are willing to do what it takes to inspire sexual purity in your child.

IN SUMMARY

Can we agree that abstinence is ultimately our children's free will decision and that we do not have the power to force it on them? Can we also agree that we have a responsibly to equip our kids with truths about sex that will protect and prepare them for the future? Finally, can we check off on the fact that we are going to have to examine our own parenting techniques before we can effectively inspire abstinence in our kids? If so, we're ready to go on to the next chapter. But first, give some thought to the following *Questions for Thought.*

Questions for Thought:

1. What is your current plan for keeping your child abstinent?

2. Is your parenting approach more like a dictator, a spectator, or a coach? Was this how you were raised?

3. How are we, as parents, setting ourselves up for failure by attempting to force abstinence on our kids?

4. Whose behavior do you focus on the most: yours or your child's?

5. When confronted with the reality of a personal character flaw, do you tend to react defensively or easily accept the need for change?

6. What in this chapter stood out to you the most and why? What do you plan to do as a result?

WARNING

I've Warned My Child — Isn't That Enough?

I have vivid memories of my third grade teacher hanging up a glossy black and white poster next to the chalkboard. The large lettered message was simple enough for an 8-year-old to read with ease—"Just say no." Unfortunately, this 1980s anti-drug campaign aimed at young people proved to be highly ineffective. Sure, the three syllable slogan cut straight to the point and fit well on kindergarteners' extra small T-shirts, but the reality is, "Just say no" just didn't work. Drug use among juveniles continued to increase despite the Reagan Administration's heartfelt efforts.

As parents, we can learn a crucial lesson from the ineffectiveness of the "Just say no" campaign. *In terms of morality, simply telling our kids not to do something is not telling them enough.*

Because I Said So!

My 4-year-old just can't understand why I want her to sit in a car seat and put up with that annoying seatbelt. It would be so much more fun for her if she could roam free in the backseat, but you and I both know that it's not safe for our kids to be unbelted. Furthermore, it's actually a gesture of love every time I buckle up my little wiggle worm.

My daughter is simply too young to really grasp how serious car accidents can be. I've explained that the seatbelt is for her safety, but she still complains about having to wear it. After I've told her over and over that it's for her own good and she continues to whine, I pull out the tried and true parental trump card: "Do it because I said so!"

In situations where we're dealing with matters that are too mature or complicated for our children to understand, "because I said so" is often the only way we believe we can combat their ongoing pleadings. But in cases where there is a way to explain the real purpose and valid reasons behind our rules, we should *always* take the time to communicate those things to our kids. As a rule of thumb, "because I said so" should be used only as a last resort.

Why, you ask? Because I said so! (Just kidding.) The real reason involves a key principle we must understand in our quest to inspire abstinence: *our convictions do not automatically become our children's convictions.* Furthermore, "because I said so" is a quick way of saying, "I have a strong belief about this that you don't possess or understand, but that's OK, just do it."

I can tell my son every day from now until he moves away to college that he should not take things that don't belong to him, but keep in mind, that does not mean that he will leave home with a personal conviction that it's wrong to steal. All these years of "because I said so" will teach him that *I* think stealing is wrong, but it will not necessarily convince *him* that it's wrong.

Convictions require being convinced, and convincing involves presenting a sound argument. "Because I said so" leaves no room for argument. Isn't that why we say it—we don't feel like arguing anymore?

A FALSE FEELING OF ASSURANCE

Most kids will admit that they know their parents don't want them having sex. Mom and Dad hear this and breathe a sigh of relief, "Our child knows not to have sex. We don't have to worry about her." Don't be so sure! Knowing they are supposed to abstain from sex doesn't mean young people plan to heed that knowledge. *We cannot make the tragic mistake of assuming that just because our children are aware of our convictions means they have also embraced them!*

In teens who report having been sexually intimate, only about half of their parents believed their teens have gone beyond kissing.[1]

I know what the speed limit is, and I know it's against the law to surpass it, but when I'm late for a hair appointment, I tend to be a little heavy footed, if you know what I mean. Case in point—knowing the rules doesn't mean we have any intention of keeping them.

One way or another, temptation is going to come to our children, and when it does, it will test the core of their belief systems. Notice what I did *not* say. I didn't say it will test *your* belief system. The temptations our kids encounter are *their* battles to fight based on *their own* core values and moral standards. It's wonderful that they know what you stand for, but it's what they stand for that ultimately counts for their well-being.

Do you remember the biblical account of little David facing off with the giant Goliath? (If you've seen the VeggieTales version, you're most likely envisioning a huge pickle right now.) Anyway, David was not even a fully grown man at the time, and King Saul was understandably concerned about the boy's ability to take on such a massive enemy. He tried to help David by loaning him his own royal armor, but it didn't fit. It was heavy and bulky, so David took it off, gave it back to Saul, and went to war with what belonged to him—his faith, a slingshot, and some stones. As it turned out, they did the trick. (See First Samuel 17.)

And so it is with us as parents. We want so badly to put our convictions on our kids so that they'll be protected in the day of battle. But our moral standards are custom made to fit *us*, not them. Our kids have to rely on *their own* convictions to defeat the giants that challenge them.

So how do young people develop convictions of their own?

CONVICTIONS DON'T COME BY HAPPENSTANCE

Wouldn't it be great if laundry would wash itself, flowerbeds never needed pruning, rolls of toilet paper simply appeared on empty dispensers, and dinner just dropped down from Heaven as soon as our families took their seats around the table? Unfortunately none of these chores happen automatically, but require on-going diligence on our part if they're going to get done.

Similarly, developing convictions in our kids doesn't just happen. We must make a constant effort to wash, prune, re-supply, and feed our kids *spiritually*, or their character and morality will stagnate. We will go on to explore how to go about this, but we must first recognize the need.

Most parents are committed to providing food, clothing, and shelter for their children, as well as emotional support, encouragement, and discipline. Do this throughout your child's upbringing, and you will raise a morally "typical" kid. And what is typical? Young people tend to be self-centered, entitled, and greedy—gifted, yet never fully satisfied with themselves or their personal accomplishments and blessings. Oh sure, there are outstanding moments when they are kind and noble, but overall, the typical modern young person is lacking in virtue.

I sat down with a mom one day who commented that she could not believe how self-centered her 18-year-old daughter had become. "She was not this way a few years ago," she complained. From the day her daughter was born, this sweet lady did a great job caring for her child's physical needs and also rallied around her education, extracurricular activities, hobbies, and goals. All the while, however, she underestimated the time, energy, and focus needed to shape the girl's spirituality and character. Now she was full of regret.

You and I can't afford to make that same mistake. Are you committed to continually investing in your child's moral development?

Ninety-one percent of teens ages 15 to 17 who have not had sex said they were motivated by keeping true to religious values.[2]

A BREAKTHROUGH WITH YOUNG PEOPLE

Over the last decade, I have ministered to kids and teenagers in a variety of circumstances and settings. I have taught from a pulpit, led small group Bible studies, and spent one-on-one time encouraging young people in the Lord. I've even ingested less than edible food at youth camps just so that I could sit at a lunch table with some kids and be a part of their conversation. Of course, I've also spent countless hours with my own children in our home.

At one point, I was convinced that adolescents and teens have very little to say to adults and even less desire to listen to what we have to say to them. Then something astonishing happened. I witnessed a breakthrough with young people that I'd never seen before. It all came to pass after the Lord showed me a profound truth. (Forgive me if it's old news to you.) *The best way to get kids to listen to you is to ask them questions. Kind of sounds like give and you shall receive, right?*

Not long after I came to terms with this truth, a sophomore in high school asked if I would lead a weekly Bible study for her and some of her friends. I quickly accepted and got to work creating lessons for the girls. I had to develop my own curriculum because I didn't see any existing material that took the approach the Lord had put on my heart.

I selected some very controversial issues that I knew were relevant to their stage of life as topics for our weekly meetings. Instead of providing the kids with an informative study sheet highlighting various Scriptures and points, I typed up questions with blank lines so the girls could write down their answers and opinions and then share them with the group if they desired.

Now when I say I typed up questions, I don't mean I asked their ages or if they know the chorus to *Amazing Grace*. I asked them some heavy questions: *What makes you think Christianity is right and other religions are wrong? How do you know the Bible is inspired by God and not man? What do you think it takes to get into Heaven? If God's so good, why do bad things happen? Does the devil really exist? Is homosexuality natural or evil? Is sex before marriage really a sin?*

From that very first meeting to the one I conducted this past week, I am thoroughly amazed at the responsiveness of the kids. If only I could bring you with me so you could see for yourself what takes place at these gatherings! I've never offered any gimmicks or prizes to get kids to come, and yet every Wednesday night 20 to 30 precious high school girls pack into their friend's living room and can't wait to get started. I pass out the question sheets, they give serious thought to their answers, and then the auctioneer-style discussion begins.

There are so many hands raised with girls waiting to ask a provocative question, share their insightful thoughts, or comment about something they've just learned, that it's a real challenge to wrap up the meeting on time and get the girls headed home. Using the Bible as our ultimate authority, they learn how very astute, relevant, and applicable God's Word is.

When I address the group to make a point, all eyes are on me, and they diligently listen. If you have a teenager, you're really not going to believe this—they even put their cell phones away! I receive their undivided attention, and they hang on my every word. Our church also conducts a group for young men, and we have found that the guys respond just as well as the girls do in this environment. In addition, we see it working beautifully in our home with our own children, which is our top priority.

The end result has been nothing short of glorious! We've watched our Bible study kids graduate and go off to college with strong convictions about who they are in Christ and where they stand on a variety of moral issues. In regard to abstinence, they know why they don't want to have sex before they're married, and they are determined in their own hearts and minds to live a life of sexual purity. They may or may not have a sexually active past, but they enter their young adult years totally convinced that physical intimacy is reserved for marriage.

FIRST STEPS TOWARD INSPIRING CONVICTIONS

What is it that we're doing in our youth small groups that is compelling young people to spend time with us, share their most personal thoughts and feelings, listen with unwavering interest, and ultimately develop their own biblically-based core values? You need to know because it's not rocket science, and it really works. Let's start with these three practical steps that can be implemented right away:

1. Know what issues are relevant to your kids.

The term *generation gap* is often used to explain the communication chasm that forms between parents and their children. The reality is, in our role as parents, we are often so caught up in our adult world (understandably) that we become totally out of touch with the issues our kids are facing every day. Oh sure, we know what subjects they struggle with in school, what nights they have extracurricular activities, and the name of their latest BFF (best friend forever). But those are just surface issues. If we're going to help build convictions in our kids, we have to seek a much deeper level of communication and connection with them.

We need to know what situations weigh on them, frighten them, excite them, and motivate them. What's on their minds? Are they worried about something, looking forward to something? *What's important in their world?*

While both parents and teens report talking to each other about sex and relationships, there appears to be a disconnect: twice as many parents than teens maintain these conversations happen often (85% to 41%).[3]

There is a way to find the answers to these kinds of questions—*ask!* Your children might give you one-word answers at first, but keep asking. In time, they will come to understand that you care about the details of their day and eventually become more vulnerable and talkative. I've provided a list of sample questions that can be used to get the ball rolling:

- ☆ Who do you sit by at lunch? What kinds of things do you talk about?
- ☆ Is there anyone at school you aren't getting along with right now? Why?
- ☆ Is there something stressing you these days?
- ☆ What are you looking forward to in this upcoming month?
- ☆ What do you like about being your age? What do you not like?
- ☆ Do you need my help with anything?
- ☆ How are you and (BFF's name) getting along?

☆ I'm all yours for the next hour. Anything you want to talk about?

Can you think of some more probing questions that apply to your child's life right now? When we know what is relevant to our kids and we take time to discuss those things with them, it goes a very long way toward establishing a beneficial rapport.

2. Be an excellent listener.

If we're going to ask our kids questions, we must be excellent listeners. In the last decade, the trend is to bring technology home with us, making it more of a challenge than ever to give undivided attention to our family members. Television, radio, cell phones, laptops, and e-mail have become a way a life for most of us. There's nothing inherently bad about this—that is, unless it drowns out quality time with our spouse and kids.

Keep in mind, *we hear with our ears but we listen with our eyes.* We must give our kids the priceless gift of our undivided attention. When was the last time you sat face to face with your child and did nothing but visit? Do you tend to do the dishes, send an e-mail, watch a football game, or fumble through junk mail while your child talks to you? And when was the last time you took your child somewhere just so the two of you could talk? If it's been a while, consider going to grab some milkshakes together or taking a walk in the park. Don't just do it once. Keep making plans to spend time talking with your child. Young children need this type of attention as well as preteens and young adults. We must show our kids that we care by putting an emphasis on quality time with them.

And when one of our kids opens up and shares something personal, we should aim to understand how he or she is feeling versus immediately launching into the brilliant solutions we have to the problem. That's not to say that we don't offer advice. It's just that we should aim to *connect* with them before we *correct* them—offer solutions and instruction only after you have acknowledged how your son or daughter feels. After all, the adage is true that people don't care how much we know until they know how much we care.

3. Ask questions that require your children to think about what they really believe.

If you have a highlighter, please get it out now and run it over this third point. This is crucial! When your child expresses some view, idea, or opinion she has about how the world works, ask her probing questions to get her thinking about the deeper things in life, such as God, human relationships, and morality.

The average young person (and adult for that matter) doesn't give enough critical thought to his or her spiritual beliefs. We hear something on the news or see someone we respect make a statement, and we tend to accept it with scarcely enough objective thought about it. *Parents, if our kids are going to develop their own convictions, we have to teach them to give serious consideration to spiritual matters.* I'll give an example to illustrate this point:

CHILD: "We learned in science class today that people came from apes. We evolved over millions of years."

PARENT: "Do you believe that?"

CHILD: "Well, I don't think my teacher and the text book would say it if it wasn't true."

PARENT: "Do you think the Bible would say something if it wasn't true?"

CHILD: "No."

PARENT: "Well if they say two different things, they can't both be right. Which one do you think is right?"

This dialog could carry on for a while! Do you see what I mean about asking questions that require our kids to give consideration to spiritual issues? Believe it or not, young people tend to really enjoy these discussions, especially if we are kind and speak in encouraging tones.

We should not use these times to intimidate our kids with how smart we are, or worse, try to prove how unintelligent they are. On the contrary, this is an opportunity to be an excellent listener and to take a sincere interest in what they believe to be true. As we come to understand what they think and feel about a particular subject, we then earn the right to share our thoughts and beliefs on issues as well.

You may be wondering if this is effective for younger children. Here is an example of an actual discussion I had with my 4-year-old daughter three days ago on our back porch. She stopped riding her big wheel just long enough to initiate this conversation.

AVERY: "I don't like the way Hannah Montana kisses one boy, then another boy, then another boy on her shows (As you are probably aware, Hannah Montana is a Disney Channel sitcom star).

ME: "Why?"

AVERY: "Because it's not right."

ME: "Why do you think it's not right?"

AVERY: "Because she should save those kisses for her husband someday."

ME: "I think that's very smart, Avery."

Why does my 4-year-old child express deep thoughts like that? First of all, it's because she hears what her older siblings say and then models after them. But it's also because my husband and I have taken the time to explain why we frown on certain behaviors. "Because I said so" is seldom spoken in our house. We also encourage our kids to answer our questions with more than *just because*. Remember, our kids must develop a habit of giving critical thought to why they believe something, not just *what* they claim as their opinion, if they are going to develop their own convictions.

Houston, We Have a Problem

In our quest to cultivate convictions in our kids, we've looked at three essential points. Additional steps are discussed throughout the upcoming chapters. In the meantime, I want to leave you with a helpful illustration.

Have you seen the movie *Apollo 13*? It's based on actual events that took place in 1970. There's a part in the film where the Apollo 13 space shuttle is orbiting the earth and its team of astronauts is reluctant about what inevitably lies ahead. They are about to temporarily lose the capacity to communicate with their ground crew at NASA. (The silent blackout has to do with the inability to send and receive a clear signal from where they will be in their rotation around the earth.) While it's never comforting to lose contact with headquarters, it is especially frightening for the Apollo 13 crew because their spacecraft is experiencing serious malfunctions. They desperately need the instruction and support of their colleagues back home, but they have no choice but to wait it out. Once they come around the far side of the earth, communication should be restored, but they wonder if they will even make it that far.

I've heard parents flippantly talk about how communication is lost with their kids during adolescent and teenage years as if a "silent blackout" is something we should expect and accept. "They'll come back around when they're older," they say with a smile. But those years just happen to be some of the most trying times in our children's lives. That's certainly not the time for them to lose contact with their support team at home. Disconnecting with our children at *any* age is no laughing matter. Furthermore, if communication is going to be restored, it must be *parents* who take the initiative to tune back into their kids. Sure, there will be seasons when they are preoccupied with other interests and clinging to their peers as their primary social outlet, but we cannot use that as an excuse to quit reaching out to them.

Adolescence is often characterized as a time of waning adult influence, a period when young people distance themselves from the values and behaviors of their elders. There is some validity to this observation, but it need not be true, nor is such a disconnect necessarily a good sign.[4]

Talk with your children, write them kind notes, send them e-mails if you have to. The key is to ask your children questions about anything and everything you can think of that might be of importance to them and then be a caring listener. Also ask provoking questions that inspire him to seek and apply spiritual truth to his life. (I have provided some tremendous resources in the endnotes of this chapter designed to equip us in biblical literacy and apologetics.)

Consider the wisdom of Second Corinthians 9:6. Let's sow bountifully into our children! In the following chapter, we'll continue to explore the practical ways that we can go about this.

He who sows sparingly will also reap sparingly, and he who sows bountifully will also reap bountifully (2 Corinthians 9:6).

Questions for Thought:

1. Why should "because I said so" be used as a last resort?

2. Are you guilty of having a false feeling of assurance regarding your child's commitment to abstinence based on his or her knowledge of your expectations, versus a personal acceptance of your standards?

3. Are you aware of what issues are most relevant to your child?

4. Do you tend to be preoccupied at home or do you consistently give your child your undivided attention?

5. Why is it important to ask our children probing questions about spiritual matters? Do you feel prepared to do this?

6. What in this chapter stood out to you the most and why? What do you plan to do as a result?

INSTILLING

Effective Abstinence Approach

Let's briefly review what we've discovered up to this point:

☆ Abstinence is ultimately my child's choice to make (I can enforce it, but cannot force it).

☆ I have a responsibility to teach my child the truth concerning sex.

☆ My child will only choose abstinence if he or she has a personal conviction to do so.

☆ Convictions will not spring up in my child by happenstance.

☆ I can start empowering my child to develop his or her own convictions by…

1. discovering and discussing the issues that are relevant to my child's needs,

2. being an excellent and caring listener, and

3. asking probing questions that provoke my child to consider spiritual matters.

The next step in our journey toward realizing the most effective approach to instilling abstinence requires that we take an honest inventory of our own spirituality.

WHAT DO MY SPIRITUAL BELIEFS HAVE TO DO WITH MY KID'S ABSTINENCE?

To answer the question posed in this subtitle— everything! You see, *abstinence is a moral decision, and morality is a spiritual issue.* If our morals are not rooted in the belief that God is watching and calling us to righteous living, then why bother conveying abstinence to our kids? We should just teach them not to get caught. Furthermore, if there are no spiritual implications to sex, we just need to make sure our kids know how to prevent disease and pregnancy and protect their reputations; then our job is done.

> [The National Campaign to Prevent Teen Pregnancy's] survey results suggest that while health information and services are an important influence on teens' decisions about sex and preventing teen pregnancy, young people's own morals and values are equally—if not more—influential.[1]

Just like the circulation of blood keeps our appendages alive, spiritual awareness is what sustains our morality. If we take God out of the equation, our morals tend to dry up and disappear. If there's no incentive bigger than ourselves by which we make decisions, no afterlife where choices made on earth have impact, then we have no real basis for doing the right thing here and now. Apart from God, the depth of our morality stops at the level of doing what it takes to spare ourselves uncomfortable consequences, and thus, not getting caught becomes the goal. Does that sound like a philosophy for shallow living to you?

DEVELOP CONFIDENCE IN YOUR OWN BELIEFS

I'm what you call "navigationally challenged." I've lived in the Houston area all of my life, and I still have to ask my husband for directions when I'm headed across town. It has become somewhat of a joke between us because he has such a keen sense of direction and I do well to find my car in the Wal-Mart parking lot! My husband says that, if I would just sit down with a road map and get thoroughly familiar with the major highways and how they run through Houston, I could make my way around town just fine. "Until you understand the big picture," he says, "you'll remain lost."

And so it is with life. As parents, we must be able to see the big picture. I'm talking about understanding how life's major issues like faith, godliness, and morality connect and operate in everyday living. When we ask our children provoking questions about spiritual issues, they are going to ask us questions in return. We don't need to pressure ourselves to have an answer for everything, but we don't want to be at a total loss for answers either. To ask our kids to give serious thought to spiritual matters, when we have never done so, is hypocritical—the equivalent of the blind leading the blind.

Mom or Dad, have you settled the anchor issues of faith in your own life? For example, do you believe God exists? Do you consider the Bible to be divinely inspired or concocted by men? Was Jesus just a good man or God in flesh sent to save humanity? What is sin? How serious is sin? Is obedience to Christ's commandments necessary? Is there one way or many ways to Heaven?

I'm sure these questions evoke responses from you, but have you really thought about how you have arrived at your conclusions? Many of us cling to various life philosophies and religious views based on bits and pieces of what someone once conveyed to us about their own beliefs—a professor, a grandparent, a television evangelist, or an outspoken childhood friend perhaps. You and I cannot afford to settle for hand-me-down spirituality; we must pursue truth for ourselves. Why not prayerfully and aggressively seek answers to your questions about faith?

If we can't explain *why* we believe something, we had better make sure we truly believe it; otherwise our professed beliefs will likely fail us should temptation or difficulties ever put them to the test. If you grew up attending church, you might mentally subscribe to certain doctrines and practices that you've heard preached over and over again, but in your heart, perhaps you don't fully understand or sincerely embrace them as truth. As a result, there's no corresponding life application. This is how we get pews full of singing Christians on Sunday mornings who live like unredeemed humanity the rest of the week. Likewise, this is why many of the young people wearing Christian T-shirts to school think nothing of taking their clothes off during dates on the weekends. We "amen" the preacher but never practice what he preaches, and a watching world concludes that our faith is nonsense—a useless waste of time.

Parents, it is of the utmost importance that we strive to resolve our own spiritual uncertainties. We'll never figure *everything* out about God and this life, but we should aim to be at peace with foundational truths, the beliefs that guide our choices in life. I encourage you to know *why* you believe and to be able to effectively explain it to someone else, specifically your child.

Christian, why do you believe in God, the salvation of His Son, and eternal life? As previously discussed, "just because," is not an effective answer, and neither is, "because the preacher said so."

If you are asked about your Christian hope, always be ready to explain it (see 1 Peter 3:15 NLT).

When we haven't settled our own spiritual perspectives and core convictions, we tend to confuse our kids. If spiritual matters are too complex or abstract for *us* to come to terms with, our kids conclude they certainly can't figure it out! They are also inclined to think, *Spirituality must not be that important if my parents are content to live without understanding it.*

Along those lines, I do not recommend that you seek to discover your core belief systems with your child as a joint effort. Oh sure, we can search out certain topics as a team, but our quest to settle our foundational beliefs should not include our children. Do you get your child to help you figure out your household finances or mediate between you and your spouse during a disagreement? I hope not! I trust you recognize that your kids are not meant to serve as your counselors. And so it is with your journey to reconcile your spiritual belief system. You need to lean on the Holy Spirit, other adults, the wealth of materials and resources available; but not your kids.

Our spiritual perspective will determine whether we attempt to instill abstinence in our kids in terms of *right and wrong or good and evil*. One approach rarely works while the other rarely fails.

RIGHT AND WRONG VERSUS GOOD AND EVIL

The account of how my great-grandparents met has been passed down through the generations in my family. Story has it that they were mere acquaintances riding together in a horse-drawn carriage when they hit a pothole and went tumbling to the ground. Horror filled my grandmother's young heart when she looked down and realized that the hem of her floor-length dress was now around her knees and her ankles were exposed! Humiliated by the scene, she turned to the blushing young man next to her and said, "Well now that you've seen my ankles, you'll have to marry me!" He did, and the rest is history.

My how times have changed. I can't relate to feeling modest about my ankles, but showing that part of the body was deemed improper in those days. Unlike today, it was a viable social stigma.

We understand that society's perception of right and wrong changes from one generation to the next. I personally am pleased that I have the liberty to wear Capri pants without apologizing for my bare ankles! However, let's not confuse the ever-changing standards of *right and wrong* with the unwavering attributes of *good and evil*. Unlike social trends, spiritual laws remain constant throughout all of history and across every culture. That's not to say that every generation and society embraces spiritual truths, but they have always been there, like an unmovable mountain since the beginning of time.

Some years ago, the Episcopal Church conducted a debate over the issue of homosexuality as an accepted or rejected lifestyle for their priests, and I happened to catch the televised event. A young woman took the floor and shared her thoughts on the subject. She waved her black Bible in the air and explained that times have changed since the Bible was written. She went on to say that many of the concepts in the Bible are old-fashioned and not applicable to modern day America.

Yikes! First she failed to acknowledge that the Bible is divinely inspired, written by the hand of mortal man but authored by an eternal God who dwells outside the limitations of time. How could anything God says become old fashioned? Second, she falsely assumed that God's Word should change to accommodate humankind's agenda instead of discerning that humankind is called to conform to the agenda set forth in God's Word.

> **All scripture is inspired by God and is useful to teach us what is true and to make us realize what is wrong in our lives. It corrects us when we are wrong and teaches us to do what is right (2 Timothy 3:16 NLT).**

That young Episcopal lady did not understand the difference between what is socially *right and wrong* and what is spiritually *good and evil*. Do you? When it comes to conveying abstinence, we must choose which approach we're going to take.

Premarital Sex in Terms of Right and Wrong

The following is an example of what we might say to a young person when we're trying to explain premarital sex as a *wrong* decision.

"Sex leads to pregnancy. It's wrong to get pregnant when you're not in a position to give a baby the life he or she deserves. Unplanned pregnancies also drastically affect a young person's college and career plans, often requiring that they take entirely different paths in life than they originally hoped and dreamed of. Obviously, waiting until you're married to start a family is best for everyone involved.

Fifty-seven percent of teens ages 13 to 17 see sex outside of marriage as morally acceptable.[2]

"Premarital sex also includes the risk of STDs, which can be painful and embarrassing or even deadly! You don't want to permanently hinder your sexual future and physical health by contracting a disease that will never leave you. Even attractive, healthy looking people carry STDs, and unless they tell you they're infected, you have no way of knowing if they are sick or not.

"One more thing, sexually active kids often get poor reputations. You don't want to be humiliated by your peers do you?"

Abstinence advocates across America do their best to steer young people away from sexual activity. They infiltrate our public school system and teach students that premarital sex is the *wrong* choice to make. Abstinence programs usually do a fantastic job explaining the gruesome symptoms that STDs inflict on their victims, and they also elaborate on the very real repercussions of teen pregnancy. They passionately warn students about the undeniable risks and consequences associated with premarital sex.

Is this approach noble? Absolutely. Is it working? Well, you saw the statistics in the first chapter. Approximately one out of every two high school students is not a virgin by the time he or she graduates. Imagine how that number climbs at the college level! Now that kids have fairly easy access to condoms and birth control pills, they assume that sex is no longer *wrong* since they are taking precautions against STDs and pregnancy. And as far as their reputation is concerned, these days it's often the girls and boys who *aren't* having sex who are teased and made fun of, not the ones having it.

Simply put, I have no confidence in presenting abstinence to kids strictly in terms of right and wrong. Kids have the tendency to conclude, "Times have changed, Mom and Dad. It may have been wrong for you, but it's not wrong for me." Furthermore, I have found that kids are willing to do the *wrong* thing on occasion, but most young people do not want to do something they know is *evil*.

PREMARITAL SEX IN TERMS OF GOOD AND EVIL

Perhaps you cringe when you hear me say we can convey sex as something good or evil because you fear I'm going to resort to religious manipulation or fear tactics. Rest assured, a *good and evil approach* simply means that our plight to instill abstinence rests on the all-important belief that there are spiritual implications to sex. Furthermore, God has a future plan and purpose for our children's sexuality. They can either forego this plan as a result of disbelief and rebellion or pursue God's plan in faith and patience.

Most strongly religious students tend to hold conservative views on sex.[3]

Do you remember the illustration Jesus gave about the man who built his house on sand while another man built his home on a rock (see Matt. 7:24-27)? The minute a storm blew in, the house constructed on sand was destroyed, whereas the home with a foundation of rock weathered the winds. Was Jesus trying to teach His audience where to build their next house? Of course not. He was conveying a spiritual reality with a natural example—unless we build our lives on the rock, Jesus Christ, we will crumble under the trials of this life (and suffer utter devastation in the next).

As we prepare to talk to our kids about sex, we must make a decision. Are we going to build on sand (right and wrong based on human reasoning) or on the rock (good and evil based on God's Word)? Several upcoming chapters elaborate on the specific spiritual implications of sex and how it relates to God's future plans for our children, and it is my goal that you feel equipped to articulate those realities. In the meantime, we must acknowledge that the best way to encourage abstinence is to do it God's way.

There is a way that seems right to a man, but in the end, it leads to death (Proverbs 14:12 NIV).

As for God, His way is perfect (Psalm 18:30).

In the following chapter, we'll look at what role the Church plays in our children's commitment to abstinence. In the meantime, I pray that you will take some time to ponder the vital questions asked of you in this chapter. They are of the utmost importance.

Questions for Thought:

1. Are your moral standards based on a belief in God or in other factors, such as family traditions or social stigmas?

2. What uncertainties do you have about religion, God, and faith? How do you suppose this is affecting your child's spirituality?

3. How do you plan to go about reconciling your spiritual uncertainties?

4. In your own words, what is the difference between a "right and wrong" and "good and evil" approach to instilling abstinence?

5. What in this chapter stood out to you the most and why? What do you plan to do as a result?

DELEGATION

Isn't it the Church's Responsibility?

Most of us are experts at delegation. We take our clothes to the dry cleaners, our pets to the groomer, our families to hairdressers, and our cars to car washes. It makes perfect sense. We don't always have the time, equipment, or training to competently do these things ourselves, but in recognizing that they must get done, we simply rely on the expertise of others to accomplish the task for us. We pay them, they complete the job, everyone is happy (except my dog—she hates being groomed).

Depending on others to take care of routine tasks is a common and useful practice in today's society. Unfortunately it's equally prevalent in modern day America for parents to delegate their children's *spiritual training* to outside sources. I use the word "unfortunately" because this tragic trend is devastating multitudes of families.

First of all, we must realize that our spirituality was never intended to be *a facet* of our lives or something we *do* on a certain day of the week. The Bible portrays Christianity as a *way of life* and the Church as something we are, not a place we go.

Too often we compartmentalize our relationship with God. We turn on our "God switch" at church on Sundays, when we bless the food at mealtimes, and sometimes at weddings and funerals when the minister leads us in prayer. But when we're at work, shopping at the mall, watching a football game, or out renting a movie, our "God switch" is off. We're not focused on God, nor are we cognizant of His leadership in our lives. This causes an *inconsistancy of character*. At church, we behave one way, but in our *real life*, outside of the sanctuary, we have totally different attitudes and priorities.

Since kids don't always do what we *say*, but nearly always do what we *do*, they inevitably emulate our example. They learn how to act one way in our presence and another way outside the home. We're often shocked when we discover certain acts of disobedience they've engaged in, but the truth is, we've modeled inconsistency of character for them. Like us, they adjust their behavior to accommodate their surroundings instead of maintaining consistent standards no matter what the circumstances may be.

When serving God is relegated to a Sunday morning experience with very little, if any, tangible application in the home, our kids do not take spiritual truths seriously. Sure, they'll play the part of a youth group member who esteems the Word of God, but when life brings a whopping temptation (as it inevitably does) they will not have the spiritual strength of character to overcome. This is where devastation can occur. A couple believes their child has a certain value system, but soon finds out, often in heartbreaking ways, that they are mistaken.

We experienced a tragedy in our extended family. One of my husband's distant cousins, a vibrant young lady in her mid-20s, was found murdered in her new home. There was also a man in the house who apparently shot her before killing himself, but none of our relatives had any idea who he was. Detectives got busy interviewing friends who knew the deceased young lady and eventually learned that the dead man was her long-time boyfriend. He had been in and out of prison and was a drug user and dealer. According to her friends, he physically and verbally abused her for years, but she went through great lengths to keep this hidden from her family. The girl's parents were shocked that she was able to conceal this abusive relationship from them, and they wondered how their daughter could live such a secret life. Her inconsistency of character was devastating to them. She was the joy of their lives, their only child.

I did not share that story to point a judgmental finger at those parents or to insinuate that they are to blame for their precious daughter's death, but rather to convey the seriousness of modeling and instilling consistency of character in our kids. As parents, we must decide if we are going to practice Christianity on occasion or devote our lives to being Christ-followers. There is a huge difference, you know. Those kids who see and understand morality and spirituality as a constant way of life are much more likely to stand strong in their core values and keep their moral commitments, such as abstinence, no matter the setting or circumstance. They see temptation as an opportunity to persevere in their beliefs rather than as an opportunity to gratify themselves.

> **Adolescents spend more time with peers and less with family. However, most teenagers' fundamental values...remain closer to their parents' than is generally realized.**[1]

CLERGY VERSUS LAITY

In the Old Testament, certain people were designated as priests, specifically those from the tribe of Levi, known as Levites. If you were not a Levite, you were not allowed to participate in priestly rituals. The New Testament, however, ushers in an entirely new standard. *All* believers are accepted as priests. (See First Peter 2:9.) You may or may not serve in fulltime ministry or hold a key leadership position in a church organization, but if you are a born-again believer, you are called to minister in some capacity based on how God uniquely designed and gifted you (see Romans 12:4-6). Perhaps you do not have the gift to articulate spiritual concepts from a pulpit, but that is irrelevant—you are a minister!

> **You are a chosen people. You are a kingdom of priests so that you can show others the goodness of God (see First Peter 2:9).**

As parents, we have been given the mandate to minister to our kids. While we are encouraged to cultivate interdependent relationships with our fellow believers (see Rom. 12:5), we are not supposed to totally rely on someone else to disciple our kids. That's right, *we are to disciple our children*, which is to say that we are to train, educate, discipline, and admonish them in God's Word. This is not a job we delegate to clergy or Sunday school teachers. While their input is valued and appreciated, you are called to take the lead in your child's spiritual growth process.

For every one parent who hears this and gets excited about the idea of ministering to his or her child, there are usually ten others who tremble with fear at the thought. "Me? I'm supposed to minister to my kid? But I don't know how, and I'm certainly not qualified!" Wait a minute. Out of all the human beings on the planet, God picked *you* to be your child's parent. He did not pick the pastor of the big church down the street or the missionary in the newsletter on your refrigerator. *He picked you.* And if He picked you, He will equip you to do what He's asking you to do.

> **And you must love the Lord your God with all your heart, all your soul, and all your strength. And you must commit yourselves wholeheartedly to these commands I am giving you**

**today. Repeat them again and again to your children...
(Deuteronomy 6:5-7a NLT).**

He is asking us to take responsibly for our children's spiritual growth and discipleship and to minister His Word to them. Here are some key points and applications that we need to know if we're going to follow through on this:

1. Quit thinking of Church as a place you go and understand it as who you are.

If you think of Church strictly as a place you go, you will never experience God in your life as He intends. As a believer in Christ, you are, quite literally, the Church! You are the conduit God intends to work through to reconcile man to Himself and to accomplish His purposes in the earth. God does not dwell in buildings, no matter how much stained glass they have. He dwells in you and me! When we understand this, we no longer compartmentalize our Christianity, which is our next point.

Don't you realize that your body is the temple of the Holy Spirit, who lives in you and was given to you by God (First Corinthians 6:19 NLT).

2. Resist the tendency to compartmentalize your Christianity.

God does not go on vacation Monday through Saturday. He is at work in and around us 24 hours a day, every day, and He is calling us to an authentic relationship that impacts *every* area of our lives. The same God who saved your soul is the same God who wants to help you with your finances, encourage you on the job, and equip you to talk to your kid about sex. In short, don't put Him in a box! *Christianity is not about inviting Christ into our lives; it's about turning our lives completely over to Him.* It's nothing He hasn't already done for us—consider the cross.

It is no longer I who live, but Christ lives in me. So I live in this earthly body by trusting in the Son of God, who loved me and gave Himself for me (Galatians 2:20 NLT).

3. Invest in your own spiritual growth.

I once invited a lady to a Bible study and her response was, "I don't need a Bible study, but my son sure could stand to go to one; he's a terror!" Keep in mind, her son was five. This lady viewed spiritual growth as something others needed, not her. Actually, we *all* need an outlet to grow and mature in our walk with God.

While I've learned from pulpit messages over the years, I have also found that I benefit a great deal from discussion-based small groups. Whereas pulpit messages allow me to simply sit and listen, small groups require that I contribute to the conversation. This motivates me to study throughout the week so that I am prepared to share knowledge and insight with my group. And if I don't understand something, I can ask questions and get feedback from the members in my group. I also enjoy the rewards of having authentic relationships with other believers who care and pray for me, just as I do for them. If you don't have a small group outlet, I encourage you to prayerfully seek one out.

4. Avoid overly relying on others to teach your child the Bible.

We often erroneously assume that we do not need to study the Bible with the same intensity and commitment level as clergy or fulltime ministers. After all, they are "called" to minister the Word. But as we've already discussed, you're called to minister the Word too! You may never stand behind a pulpit, but do you carry on conversations with co-workers? Do you spend time with friends on the golf course or visit with ladies at the salon? These are all opportunities that God can use for ministry. We must be prepared to share God's Word any time He brings someone across our path who expresses a spiritual need, starting with our kids.

While it's not likely that our kids are going to plop down next to us on the couch and say, "Mom and Dad, I have a spiritual need today," the fact that they are young is indicative of the reality that they are in continual need of spiritual guidance. And if we're going to minister, we need to know what the Bible says. Unfortunately, biblical literacy is not high on our nation's priority list right now, but it doesn't have to be that way in your home. Get a version of the Bible that's easiest for you to read, and get started, preferably in the New Testament Gospels if you are new to reading your Bible. There are all sorts of resources available to help us learn God's Word; we just have to make the effort (see Chapter Three endnotes for recommended resources).

5. Discuss God's Word with your child.

As parents, our goal should be to spark discussions about God's principles with our children. We can do this during times that we've set aside specifically for the purpose of looking at God's Word with them or spontaneously in the midst of our everyday interactions with our kids—in the car or at the dinner table, for example.

When our children are toddlers and in early elementary school, we can tell them Bible stories, and then ask questions regarding the plot and key points of the stories. In doing this, we train them to do more than read the Bible; they learn to think about its message. As our kids grow into older elementary students, we can venture beyond the stories and into the passages that deal with life principles, such as those we find in Proverbs, for example. As we read the Word with them, we should continually ask if they understand how the passages of Scripture apply to their lives.

> Repeat [God's commandments] again and again to your children. Talk about them when you are at home and when you are away on a journey, when you are going to bed and when you are getting up....Write them on the doorposts of your house and on your gates (Deuteronomy 6:7,9).

By the time our kids are high school students, it can be very helpful to do topical studies in which we take a specific topic based on the issues most relevant to them, such as dating, gossip, faith, love, or sex, and talk about what the Bible says concerning those matters. There are a great variety of age-specific devotionals available to guide us in biblical discussions with our kids, which can be very helpful.

While I do think it is worthwhile to encourage kids to memorize Scripture, I feel it is of even greater importance to make sure they know how to correctly apply biblical principles to their lives in everyday settings. It can be said that Scripture memorization puts tools in our children's toolboxes, while discussions about God's Word equip them to skillfully put the tools to use.

I'm Not Worthy To Teach My Kid About Abstinence

You may find what I'm about to say a little shocking since I am the author of a book about inspiring abstinence.

I did not wait until I was married to have sex. I got pregnant when I was 20, married the father of my child in hopes of salvaging the situation, experienced abandonment and a painful divorce two years later, and found myself raising a daughter alone at 22 years of age. It was at that very low point in my life that I realized that it was time to start doing things God's way. I suddenly understood that He was not attempting to take away my fun when He declared that sex is reserved for marriage. God's intent was to spare me the heartache of the very circumstances in which I found myself.

As a young girl, I understood that Jesus died for my sins, but I had never acknowledged Him as *Lord*, which is to say, I had never allowed Him to be the leader of my life. But at 22 years of age, I drew a proverbial line in the sand and decided it was time to follow Him. Based on the truth found in His Word, I started doing things *His* way for a change. Sometime later, I met my future husband,

and we *did* wait until we were married to become physically intimate. Honestly, it wasn't easy, but I had learned my lesson about doing things *my* way. This time, I was going to honor God with every area of my life, including my love life.

If you've had a promiscuous past, you may wonder if you have the right to talk to your child about abstinence. Allow me to answer that question in a single word—*yes!* There's no shame in imparting truths to our kids in an effort to keep them from walking into the same traps and snares that we did. I have never tried to lie to my kids about my past. While I have spared them the particular details, my two oldest children have heard my testimony and understand that I want abstinence for them because I know what it's like to rebel against God in that area. Our kids appreciate honesty.

Don't let condemnation over your past stop you from confidently communicating with your child. Instead, let your failed life experiences be the catalyst that motivates you to inspire abstinence in your son or daughter.

Please take note that I said, "Don't let condemnation over your *past* stop you." It's quite a different story if you are still trapped in sexual sin. How can we possibly inspire sexual purity in our children if we are currently addicted to pornography or engaging in sex outside of marriage? I must warn you, you will do a great deal of damage to your children if you convey a message of abstinence when they know full well that you are not in control of your own sexual appetites. Even if we think our habits are well hidden from our kids, we have no idea how much they actually know or will soon find out. Whether we have young children or older teens, they can readily pick up on hypocrisy, and they always resent it. The old adage, "Do as I say but not as I do," is a formula for disaster!

If you find yourself overcome by a sinful habit involving sexual deviance, the Bible takes all the guesswork out of how to get free from its grip. It's not something we particularly like to do, but it is crucial if we're going to overcome it. In addition to repenting of our sin to God, we must find a mature Christian to whom we can confess our sin. From there, we should afford that person the liberty to hold us accountable in that area. We may need a licensed Christian counselor or simply a friend in the faith who is wise and full of the Word, depending on how entrenched we are in the ordeal. Remember, this can't be someone who will simply feel sorry for us, say a little prayer, and be done. We need someone who will continually look us in the face and remind us how serious sin is and how available God's loving grace is to help us in times of temptation. We should be able to contact this person day or night if we are feeling overwhelmed by temptation and are in need of encouragement and support.

Confess your sins to each other and pray for each other so that you may be healed. The earnest prayer of a righteous person has great power and produces wonderful results (James 5:16 NLT).

There are also practical things we should do to avoid temptation, such as installing stringent filters and accountability programs on our home Internet connection if online pornography is a problem we battle.

IS THERE ANOTHER WAY?

Jesus pled, "My Father! If it be possible, let this cup of suffering pass by me" (Matt. 26:39). He was praying that, if there was any other way to save humanity, God would spare Him the horror and shame of the cross. We know what happened next. Jesus went through the very agony He dreaded, and He suffered horrific beatings and death by crucifixion. God's response to Christ's prayer is obvious, "My Son, there is no other way."

When it comes to ministering to our children, God is not going to *let this cup pass by us.* He isn't going to provide *another way* that relieves us of the responsibility to cultivate spiritual convictions in them, including abstinence. Furthermore, *instilling abstinence in our children is a discipleship issue.*

Perhaps God will use an outlet outside the home to influence our kids in the right direction spiritually, but that in no way entitles us to shrink back from our God-given parental duties, nor does it excuse any apathy we may have. Children and youth ministers typically speak into our children's lives about a half-hour a week; their ability to influence our children in this limited amount of time pales in comparison to the daily, ongoing opportunity we have to cultivate godly values in our children at home.

> **It doesn't take much sacrifice to drop our kids off at youth group, but it will surely require some major adjustments on our part to disciple our kids.**

> **Children who discuss sex with their parents take fewer risks, avoid pressure to have sex, and think that their parents provide good information.[2]**

We've been given stewardship over our kids, which means that we will stand before God and give account for how we chose to invest in them. While our culture is obsessed with investing in children's education, extracurricular activities, and extensive wardrobes, God is calling us to devote our time, energy, and resources to our children's *spiritual growth.* It doesn't take much sacrifice to drop our kids off at youth group, but it will surely require some major adjustments on our part to disciple our kids through home Bible studies and family devotion times.

Immediately following Christ's request for the Father to *let the cup pass by Him,* He lovingly prayed, "Nevertheless, your will be done, not mine" (see Matt. 26:39). Is that the prayer in your heart today? If so, you are ready to proceed to the following chapter of this book, where we'll examine how our family relationships and home environment affect our children's sexuality.

Questions for Thought:

1. Before now, have you taken the lead role in discipling and spiritually maturing your child? Why or why not?

2. Explain "compartmentalized Christianity" in your own words. What are the potential repercussions of having compartmentalized Christianity?

3. As a parent, do you feel you model consistency of character for your child? If not, what adjustments need to be made?

4. Are you adequately investing in your own spiritual growth? How might you make a bigger investment?

5. Do you feel comfortable teaching your child about the Bible? What is your greatest obstacle and how can it be overcome?

6. What in this chapter stood out to you the most and why? What do you plan to do as a result?

5

HOME LIFE

What Affects a Child's Sexuality?

Newborn babies are the epitome of innocence, aren't they? They enter the world with a totally clean slate, with no history of hurting anyone or anything. They are also born with absolutely no sense of self or a personal identity. A baby's eyes are focused for hours a day on his parents' faces and the colorful world around him, not on his own appearance or stature. As he grows, he develops an idea of who he is based solely on what he is told about himself and how his caregivers convey his value and worth. This provides parents the wonderful opportunity to write beautiful messages on the blank canvas of their children's hearts. Unfortunately, it also makes it possible for hard-hearted individuals to carve painful impressions, leaving their children feeling worthless and wounded at the core of their being.

It is my observation that kids adopt one of three general identities depending on how they have been treated and spoken to early in life.

1. "I am valuable."

Children who are shown continual affection and verbal affirmation, combined with healthy doses of discipline, develop a personal sense of value and worth. When their home environment is loving, safe, and free from parental strife, kids form a relatively healthy view of themselves.

2. "I am a burden."

When children are born into a volatile home-life that consists of ongoing arguing, cruel name-calling, flaring tempers, and unstable relationships, they conclude they are a burden (children have the uncanny ability to blame all of the problems that take place around them on themselves). If children are physically, verbally, or sexually abused, the notion of being a burden is driven into the deepest recesses of their heart. As a result, they will battle feelings of insecurity, worthlessness, and inferiority all of their life unless their childhood wounds are identified and ministered to. Without intervention, it is also likely that they will repeat the dysfunction of their childhood and inflict similar wounds on their kids someday.

3. "I am invisible."

Unlike the child made to feel like a burden due to his or her parents' negative attention, this child's wound is the result of *not enough* parental attention. Parental neglect can manifest in the form of unmet physical needs or abandonment, but is often due to factors as subtle as parents' career demands or preoccupied lifestyles. Perhaps a child's parents are hardworking professionals, successful community leaders, or prominent pastors for that matter. Then again, the child may have a single mom who has no choice but to work long hours, and cannot help the fact that she is frequently not home. Whatever the case, a lack of attention, quality time, discipline, and parental interaction conveys the painful message to a child that he or she is nothing special and not worthy of the parents' time or energy. This causes a child to feel depressed, worthless, and desperate for recognition, which, more often than not, drives him or her to *unhealthy* sources of attention.

IDENTITY TYPE INFLUENCES SEXUAL BEHAVIOR

It's been said that all males have a certain question regarding their manhood that demands an answer. Likewise, all females crave a response to a particular question about their own femininity and identity. Our gender-specific question nags at our hearts from early childhood and continues throughout our lives, especially if we get a negative response or no response at all during our formidable years.

According to John and Staci Elderedge, for boys, the question is: *"Do I have what it takes to be a man?"* For girls, the question is, *"Am I lovely?"*[1]

When the family relationships and early life experiences of children convey a resounding "no" to their most vulnerable questions, or if there is a lack of affirmation one way or the other, the children do the one thing that comes natural—*search for someone to give them the response they crave.* A young person may turn to a local gang for acceptance and validation or a loving Sunday school teacher, depending on who reaches out to him first. His allegiance will lie with whoever answers "yes" to his heart's question, even if this affirmation comes from a deceptive, manipulative source.

Young people operating out of a broken identity are on a desperate hunt for validation, and premarital sex can be a very alluring outlet.

Why insecure young men seek affirmation through premarital sex:

I was in the grocery store check-out line the other day and two teenage boys in line behind me were carrying on a conversation. One of the boys abruptly changed the topic of their discussion, sports, to comment about a magazine cover on the shelf in front of him. Apparently he noticed the headlines—a prominent actress and sex symbol was pregnant. The young man commented to his friend, "Wow, that's a lucky guy who knocked her up!" His statement was heartbreaking, but not at all a surprise. Manhood is often erroneously defined by a man's ability to "conquer" a female, and the sexier she is, the greater the "score."

I never went into the boys' locker room in high school, but I heard my share of rumors that originated there. Guys would brag and swap stories about who they fooled around with and how physically far they managed to get. The bigger breasted the girl, and the more a young man was able to coax her into doing, the more accolades he received from his peers. In such cases, every pat on the back and sigh of envy communicates one thing to an insecure boy, "Yes, I *do* have what it takes to be man!"

A young man's ability to manipulate a girl into having sex hardly exemplifies biblical manhood, but with no knowledge of such truths, his conquests with females make him feel like a man. Sex becomes the outlet he relies on to bolster his own distorted sense of self-confidence.

> **In a national survey, nearly one-third of 15-to-17 year olds, especially boys, said they had experienced pressure to have sex.**[2]

Why insecure young women seek affirmation through premarital sex:

I really take offense when high school girls refer to another girl as a "slut." Not only is it a cruel and derogatory word, but I don't believe there are any young girls who are capable of being such a thing. Are there girls who are so desperate for attention that they will give their bodies to one boy after another in hopes of feeling loved? Yes. But I have yet to meet a teenage girl who sleeps around simply for the purpose of sexual gratification. It's always about getting her question answered—*Am I lovely?*

Seventy-five percent of teen girls 15 to 19 agree that society tells girls that attracting boys and acting sexy are some of the most important things girls can do.[3]

A guy looking to take advantage of a girl sexually knows exactly what kind of female to target and just what to say her. He's on the lookout for an attractive girl who feels worthless. He knows that, if he tells her she means the world to him ("You are lovely to me!"), she'll most likely surrender her body. When he takes her physical intimacy, dumps her, and then brags about his victory to his schoolmates, it only drives home what she has always believed, *"No, I am **not** lovely."*

MOM AND DAD'S ROLE

As parents, we are the central relationship in our children's lives that influences their identities. Both a mother's *and* a father's influences are vital in a child's life. Knowing this, let's now look at how they each operate according to our kids' specific gender (whether you are a mom or a dad, I recommend that you read the father and mother explanations below).

How a father impacts his daughter's identity:

I've spent countless hours listening to teenage girls' hurts and desires, and this experience has led me to a certain conclusion—*girls need their dads **just as much** as they need their moms.* While there is a great deal a mother can do to answer her daughter's question, "Am I lovely," a little girl longs to have a man answer this question (i.e., her father). No matter how much a mother dotes on her daughter or affirms her beauty (inside and out), young girls desire to be affirmed by a man. Perhaps women's liberation advocates would be offended at this logic, but I'm guessing such women have never been in the position of handing tissues to sobbing girls who want, more than anything, for their fathers to notice them.

The absence of a father, especially early in a young person's life, is a strong factor associated with adolescent sexual activity.[4]

Dad, you simply must take the time to tell your daughter how smart she is, how unique and gifted she is, and how truly *lovely* she is. You may do a superb job paying the bills, providing her with health insurance, and carpooling her to and from extracurricular actives, *but what are you **saying** to her, about her?*

A wise man once said, "Sometimes silence is golden, and sometimes it's just plain yellow!" Case in point, don't withhold the affection and verbal affirmation your daughter so desperately needs. Of all the factors that will influence her identity, *you* are key.

How a dad impacts his son's identity:

It's no coincidence that fatherlessness is becoming a worldwide epidemic at an exponential rate. Our spiritual enemy understands that removing fathers from the home is a deathblow to the family. While women courageously rise to the challenge of single motherhood, let us not overlook the value of having dad in the picture. You see, no matter how hard she tries, mom cannot answer her son's question, "Do I have what it takes to be a man?" Sure, she can instill godly values of manhood in him, but *only a man* can affirm a boy's manhood.

Little boys are pre-wired for masculinity but are not born with an innate confidence that they are, in fact, masculine. It is only as a father confirms their manhood that boys begin to *feel* manly. "Way to go, sport!" "Try again—you've got what it takes, son." "Yes, you *are* strong." These kinds of affirming statements from a masculine source satisfy a young boy's need to be viewed as manly.

When a father is overly critical or belittling, a boy will exhaust himself trying to gain his father's approval. Conversely, when a father is the strong silent type that rarely engages his son or takes an active interest in him, a boy perpetually seeks to discover what it is about himself that is so unacceptable—perhaps if he can somehow change himself, his father will desire to know and love him.

Despite all the media hype and opinions circulating about homosexuality today, research shows that homosexuality in males is the result of a young man having never been made to feel masculine in the formidable years of early childhood (i.e., no manly affirmation from a father-figure).[5] Some experts assert that masculinity is the God-given desire in *every* boy's heart, but when masculinity eludes him, a boy will erroneously conclude that manhood, for him, is unattainable. His infatuation with being masculine subsequently results in being attracted to masculinity (homosexuality).[6]

Dad, your son needs you! He needs is to hear you say you are proud of the *man* he's becoming. He needs you to answer his soul's question, "Do I have what it takes to be a man?" From there, teach him how to respect young ladies and guard his sexual appetite. Show him how manhood is truly defined—not by sexual exploits but by Christ-likeness!

Some parents use a double-standard, warning their daughters of sexual dangers while encouraging experimentation by their sons.[7]

How a mother impacts her daughter's identity:

I was recently at a little league football event and began chatting with several of the moms. Having two daughters myself, I was shocked and horrified by what I kept hearing mothers say about their little girls, right in front of their little girls! "My boys are so much easier." "Girls are a pain in the butt." "My son is very independent, but this one (pointing to her 3-year-old daughter) is too clingy; she drives me crazy!"

Daughters are a tremendous gift; unfortunately not all mothers recognize the blessing they have been given. *As mothers, we have the unique ability to validate the nurturing spirit in our daughters.*

We do this by conveying that their femininity is precious and valuable—not shameful or irritating.

Girls often struggle to make sense of their emotions, which can equate to emotional ups and downs, also known as "mood swings." For parents, this can be exhausting at times, but let us not send the message to our daughters that their emotional make up is a nuisance or disgraceful quality! On the contrary, let's teach them how to manage their emotions while preserving and celebrating their God-given sensitivity.

Teenagers who have close, warm relationships with their mothers are more likely to delay sexual activity.[8]

When a mother is jealous, intolerant, or contentious toward her daughter, the implied answer to her daughter's question, "Am I lovely," is, "No, you are too much to deal with!" Now compare this with the message a manipulative young man is likely to tell the girl, "Baby, you are the most beautiful thing I've ever seen!" A young woman desperately seeking validation will be vulnerable to the attention and flattery that accompanies sexual relationships. Mothers, we can help safeguard our daughters from relying on unhealthy forms of attention by embracing them for who they are and being patient and supportive during the adolescent and teen years, when our daughters are coping with the ongoing challenges of hormone fluctuations and emotional swings.

How a mother impacts her son's identity:

If you want to make a boy angry, just say something ugly about his mother! As a general rule, guys tend to hold their mothers in high esteem. Her nurturing spirit is refreshing to his soul and endears him to her. Because he values her so, a mother typically has a great deal of influence in her son's life, which provides her with a wonderful opportunity to impart wisdom, godliness, and spiritual maturity to her son. While this loving investment goes a long way toward shaping his manhood, only a man can answer a boy's primary question, "Do I have what it takes to be a man?" This is not due to female incompetence, but rather, due to the fact that a boy's need to be affirmed in his masculinity necessitates that validation comes from a masculine source.

One of the ways women can seriously stifle their sons' character development is by being dominating and overbearing. Women who rip the proverbial pants off their husbands and wear them around the house with pride not only trample their husbands' masculinity, but their sons' as well. The same dysfunction occurs when single moms continually express bitterness and cynicism about men in front of their sons. "Men are good for nothing." "Leave it to a man to mess things up." "If your father wasn't such an idiot, we wouldn't be in this mess!"

When a boy finds himself in an atmosphere where his mom dominates his dad or degrades men, it is as if his mother responds to his heart's question, "Do I have what it takes to be a man," by saying, "No, I'll be the man for you!" Just like birds need open air in order to spread their wings and fly, males need an environment where they are free to express their manhood and be respected as masculine beings. A dominating woman "clips her son's wings" before he ever leaves the nest, and as a result, he is at a disadvantage when it comes time to leave home and soar alongside other men. Furthermore, his broken identity makes him vulnerable to using premarital sex as an outlet to assert his manhood. His ability to "conquer" and satisfy a girl sexually makes him feel strong—a stark contrast from the "weakling" he often feels like at home.

How parents working together impact their children:

Adolescents who live with both biological parents are less than half as likely to begin a sexual relationship as those who don't.[9]

As it pertains to child rearing, it could be said that a father stabilizes his child while a mother nourishes her child, creating an ideal balance of *fortifying* and *feeding* their child's spirit and soul. Men are called to be the head of their families (see Eph. 5:23); I like to say that women are called to be the heart. What a beautiful partnership! Both are vital and serve each other while working harmoniously to keep their home healthy and flourishing.

As of 2008, the most rapidly increasing family structure in the United States is single Dads. Tragically, multitudes of women are abandoning their husbands and children to go "find themselves." In cases where a mother or father simply cannot be involved in his or her children's lives for whatever reason, it's imperative that we seek out a loving relative, friend, or fellow church member who would like to serve as a godly role model and source of affirmation for our children.

CREATING A HEALTHY MORAL ATMOSPHERE

Our spiritual enemy is on a mission to exploit our children's sexuality as early in their lives as possible. Knowing this, the *moral atmosphere* in our homes is instrumental in either provoking or protecting our children's sexual appetites. Consider the following illustration.

The Trojan Horse

If you studied Greek mythology in school, you will most likely recall the infamous Trojan horse in Virgil's Latin epic poem, *The Aeneid.* According to the tale, the Greeks wanted to bring about the demise of the city of Troy, so they developed an ingenious covert operation. The Greeks pretended to sail away, leaving one man behind to present Troy with an enormous wooden horse. He told the Trojans that the horse was an offering and that, if they would receive it into their city, they would have the "good fortune" they needed in order to defeat the Greeks. Ignoring the adamant warnings from their priest, the Trojans accepted the gift and brought the massive structure into their heavily fortified city. You probably recall what happened next—at nightfall, thousands of Greek warriors poured out of the wooden horse and slaughtered the unsuspecting Trojans.

While I do not believe in the tales of Greek mythology, I do believe the Trojan horse illustrates a powerful military strategy that our spiritual enemy knows all too well. Satan is an expert at trespassing into unsuspecting Christian households and destroying families from within. He accomplishes this through highly esteemed, seemingly innocent household items—*our media outlets.*

Consider the following facts, according to the National Coalition for the Protection of Children and Families:[10]

☆ Seventy-five percent of prime time television in the 1999-2000 season included sexual content.

☆ Over 80 percent of shows popular with teens contain sexual content, a rate higher than shows for other audiences. Only 15 percent of sexual encounters on TV alluded to the possible risks or responsibilities of sexual activity.

☆ Adolescents who watch television with high levels of sexual content are *twice as likely* to initiate sexual intercourse and also more likely to initiate other sexual activities.

☆ Teens with high levels of exposure to rap videos, which often promote drug use, violence and sex, are significantly more likely to acquire an STD.

☆ Movies have an 87 percent likelihood of presenting sexual material.

☆ Seventy percent of sexual advances over the Internet happened while youngsters were on a home computer.

☆ The average age of first Internet exposure to pornography is 11 years old.

☆ The largest consumer of Internet pornography is the 12-17 age group.

STAND GUARD

Parents, the conclusion is obvious. We must guard our kids against the toxic media influences that vie for their attention through avenues such as television programs, movies, Internet activity, magazines, and music. Are you familiar with the lyrics to the songs your child is committing to memory from his or her iPod?

In my home, we have a "no compromise" agreement. For example, if a television show involves sexual images, innuendoes, coarse jesting, or any *hint* of sexually stimulating material, whoever has the remote changes the channel. As you can imagine, this greatly limits the programs we are able to view, but last time I checked, no one has died for lack of watching a popular television show. There are plenty of young people, however, being poisoned by what they *are* watching.

> **Unfortunately, many teenagers get much of their "sex education" from the media, which present a distorted view of sexual activity, associating it with fun, excitement, competition, danger, or violence, and rarely showing the risks of unprotected sex.[11]**

My family's media standards may be considered extreme to some, but my husband and I aren't going to apologize that we are *extremely* passionate about protecting our children's sexual purity.

As is our custom, we've taken the time to help our kids understand why we maintain certain boundaries. Rather than telling our kids they can't watch a particular television program simply because it's "bad," we discuss the specific quality of the show that we find offensive and tie in the biblical principles that apply to the situation. As a result, our kids often change the channel during inappropriate programs of their own volition before we even have to say anything.

Does your child have a television or computer in the bedroom? We have to be especially careful about media outlets that provide kids with large amounts of unsupervised access. Even kids with the best of intentions can accidentally turn on a television program or log onto a site that is not appropriate.

What about television shows that have no nudity but contain sexual innuendoes and coarse jesting? This can also plant seeds of perversion in our kids' hearts and undermine the sacredness of sex. Not only do my husband and I forbid our kids to watch such shows, but we don't watch them either—remember, kids are inclined to do what we *do*, not what we just *tell* them to do.

Teens with high levels of exposure to rap videos, which often promote drug use, violence, and sex, are significantly more likely to acquire an STD.[12]

My kids don't exactly celebrate when they have to pass up going to a particular movie with friends due to inappropriate content, but then again, I didn't celebrate today when I had to walk away from a group of moms who were gossiping outside my daughter's preschool class. Case in point, as long as we're serving Christ, there will be times we must separate ourselves from certain social situations.

If your aim is to enjoy this world, you can't be a friend of God (see James 4:4b).

Enact a Plan

Why not have a family discussion tonight and collaborate about what your household will and will not allow into your home in the form of media? Also, decide what monitoring methods you are going to establish to keep an eye on your kid's media choices. Using Ephesians 5:3 as your standard, as well as the rest of the Bible's wisdom, set some clearly defined boundaries, and then stick to them! Don't allow the humor of a certain sitcom or the "overall plot" of an intriguing movie to be your excuse for compromising.

But among you there must not be even a hint of sexual immorality, or of any kind of impurity...because these are improper for God's holy people (Ephesians 5:3 NIV).

On more than one occasion, my husband and I have had to take movie rentals right back to the store after the first scene because they violated the moral standard of our home. We didn't get our money back, but we *did* maintain our kids' respect.

Parents, let's model an unwavering commitment to moral purity for our kids so that they understand what it means to resist compromise. Just think, someday they'll set the standard for what our grandchildren are watching.

What If We've Made Mistakes?

Throughout this chapter, we've looked at some of the tremendous responsibilities we have as parents and how our decisions directly impact our children. While it can be painful to arrive at the conclusion that we have made certain mistakes, we must be willing to examine our parenting and repent when we discover an area where we have fallen short of God's mandates. The process for repenting involves:

If we confess our sins, He [God] is faithful and just to forgive us our sins and to cleanse us from all unrighteousness (1 John 1:9).

1. Acknowledging the specific way we have failed to meet God's standard (versus making excuses or justifying our actions)

2. Asking God to forgive us

3. Forgiving ourselves, which means letting go of any guilt or self disrespect we've been carrying

4. Repenting to our kids if we have hurt or wounded them

Parents sometimes wonder, "Will my kids still respect me if I admit my mistakes to them?" The answer is not only *yes*, but it's important to also note that our kids actually *lose* respect for us when we are too proud to repent for our wrongdoing. How much would it have meant to you growing up if your parents would have asked for your forgiveness after having hurt you in some way?

Are you aware of having said or done something that may have had a negative impact on your child's identity and personal sense of value? Have you failed to say enough to your child about his or her worth? Perhaps you have not taken a strong enough stance against illicit media influences in your home, and your child has been exposed to damaging images or sexually arousing television programs. I'd like to suggest offering up the following prayer to God and then repenting, if need be (something I must do on a regular basis).

"Father, I acknowledge that children are a gift from you and that You have entrusted me with a tremendous responsibility. Lord, please show me where I have failed to be the Christ-like example, influence, and authority You have called me to be. Open my eyes to the ways I may unknowingly be wounding or misleading my child, and grace me by Your spirit to change. Empower me to train up my child in Your ways so that he (or she) is equipped to do what You have called him (or her) to do for Your Kingdom. Give me the humility to admit where I've missed Your mark, and the encouragement to grow and mature as a parent. Father, I now repent for ... "

"In Jesus' name I pray. Amen."

Questions for Thought:

1. Out of the three identity types described in this chapter, which one do you think you are cultivating in your child? Do you need to make any adjustments or changes?

2. How do you feel you are responding to your child's most pressing question ("Do I have what it takes to be a man?" or "Am I lovely?")?

3. Is your child lacking affirmation from a mother or father figure? Is there anyone you know who could serve as a mentor in your child's life?

4. Do the media standards in your home protect your child's sexual appetite? If not, what do you plan to do about it?

5. What in this chapter stood out to you the most and why? What do you plan to do as a result?

TIMING

How Old for Sex Talk?

The earlier we start inspiring sexual purity in our kids, the better. Believe it or not, we can begin preparing them to embrace abstinence long before they are mature enough to discuss sex. How? By helping our kids to understand that God has set apart a mate especially for them and that that person is worth waiting for. Our kids should grow accustomed to the notion that there is one person—*just one*—who is deserving of their romantic love.

We can begin planting seeds of abstinence in our kids even if they are just toddlers. It all begins with prayer. When we tuck our little ones into bed, that's a great time to pray with them, and more specifically, to pray for their future mates. Here's an example of the way I've been praying with each of my daughters over the years:

"Lord, I thank you that you are preparing a godly, handsome mate for my daughter. I pray that he is becoming more and more like Christ every day. Give his parents the wisdom to instill your principles in his heart so that he will know how to love, honor, and cherish my daughter someday. And help me to teach my daughter how to love and forgive so that she too will be a Christ-like spouse. I thank you that when the timing is right, You will lead them to each other and they will know Your will for their lives."

The following factors may play a part in an adolescent's decision to become sexually active: early entrance into puberty, poverty, poor school performance, lack of academic and career goals, a history of sexual abuse or parental neglect, and cultural or family patterns of early sexual experience.[1]

Whether your children are toddlers or teenagers, it is crucial that they hear you pray for their future spouse on a regular basis. In doing so, you are cementing the idea in your child that there is *one* person out there for him or her and that that person is so cherished and precious that your child can anticipate a relationship with that future spouse years in advance. In this way, children come to understand that they are waiting for their future spouse even before they are old enough to comprehend the sexual aspect of that wait.

It doesn't take long, however, for our kids to realize that not everyone lives as if there's only *one* lover for them. Just watching Disney Channel will open their eyes to this. Our kids see their most admired child stars chase one member of the opposite sex after another and lock lips with a different young person from one episode to the next. The only prerequisite for pursuing a love interest is whether or not a guy or girl is "hot."

Eventually our kids start school and witness girls and boys swapping boyfriends and girlfriends like baseball cards. While there's nothing overtly evil about this kind of behavior, we should teach our kids that God has a better way—they don't have to kiss a dozen frogs to find their prince!

Keep in mind, our kids should never be made to feel guilty for developing a crush on someone. Attraction is a natural part of life and any healthy young person will feel drawn toward certain members of the opposite sex. At times my children proceed to tell me, in great detail, how cute a certain guy or girl is, and I affirm their emotions. However, my kids understand the difference between *feeling attraction* and *taking action* (more about this in our chapter about dating).

By the time our kids are progressing through elementary school, we should encourage them to save their hugs and kisses for their future mates. *Don't ever underestimate a child's ability to understand the need to wait until they are married to express romantic affection.* Once our children know that God has one special mate for them, we can use the situations they're confronted with by their peers to spark great discussions—"I know all of your friends are kissing girls behind the monkey bars, but would you want *your* future wife doing that?" God has given each of us an innate sense of protectiveness, a godly jealousy of sorts that naturally arises when we have a romantic love for someone. Amazingly, even children can identify with this on a certain level.

Please understand that I am in no way advocating creating an odd obsession in our kids so that they become angry someday if they find out their fiancé did, in fact, kiss a boy behind the monkey bars in elementary school! At the same time, let us not be so influenced by our culture that we become desensitized to God's standards. As we will see in the following chapter, *acts of physical intimacy are part of the covenant ritual of marriage and are designed to bond two people together for life.* For this reason, I personally don't think it's cute when two kids hide under the bleachers and "make out." I'm teaching my kids that romantic affection is sacred. I'm also teaching them *why* so that they can embrace God's standards for themselves and focus on what they have to look forward to, versus what they are giving up.

THE PRETEEN YEARS

There is no official age that indicates it's time to talk to our kids about sex. However, as a general rule, puberty tends to spark sexual curiosity, so our kids' bodily changes can serve as an obvious sign that we need to start discussing sexuality with them. Keep in mind, some kids will think sex is gross, but since we know their attitude will change dramatically one day in the not-so-far future, we need to instill godly perspectives in our sons and daughters, even if, at the time, they are disgusted by the topic.

> **The best [abstinence] programs start before high school, include assignments that require parent-child communication, focus on behavior and not just information, and last for years.[2]**

Our culture is so sexually explicit that our kids may know more about sex than we think they do. It is highly likely that by the time they are in middle school, they've been exposed to all kinds of sexually based conversations and stories from their peers, if not actual propositions. For this reason, we cannot afford to wait until our kids are in their late teens to start talking to them about sex.

> **The average girl has her first sexual intercourse at 17, the average boy at 16, and approximately 25 percent of boys and girls report having had intercourse by age 15.[3]**

If we've reared our kids with the knowledge that God is preparing a mate especially for them, it makes for a smooth transition into discussions about valuing virginity when they are old enough to learn about sex. They already understand the idea of waiting for their mate; now they just have another aspect added to that wait—sexual activity.

If our kids are teens before we start encouraging the idea of setting their sights on the one mate God has in mind for their future, there's no need to fret; better later than never.

THE SEX TALK

It's important that we renew our minds against the notion of having "the sex talk," as if we discuss sex one time with our kids and then we're done. Sex is something we should talk about with our children throughout their upbringing. As they grow in maturity, we can expand on the depth and detail we share.

Eighty-seven percent of teens ages 12 through 19 say it would be easier to postpone sexual activity if able to have more open, honest conversations with parents.[4]

Sometimes children have questions about sex before they are mature enough to comprehend the answers. When my oldest daughter was in the second grade, she glanced up from her homework one afternoon and casually asked me, "Does Dad like to see you naked?" I was shocked! I told her I valued her question, but I wanted to wait until she was a little older before I gave her an answer. (I also needed time to catch my breath!) I prayed about what to say and sometime later, I introduced the concept of sex to my daughter without going into much detail— "God made our bodies so that when two people are married, they fit together perfectly and it feels good to be this close to each other." This of course sparked additional questions, to which I gave more specific answers as she got older.

Our children's questions about sex will not go unanswered; the issue is: *who will provide them with answers?* If our kids start asking us questions about sex, we want to do our best to respond with truthful information; otherwise they'll ask someone else who will give them the *wrong* answers.

If you feel your child is too immature to understand sexuality or if he's caught you off guard and you need time to collect your thoughts, it's OK to explain that you will answer at a later time. Just make sure you affirm the fact that he came to you with his questions and that there's nothing wrong with wondering about that sort of thing. It's crucial that our kids feel comfortable coming to us with their uncertainties about sex. It's also essential that we do, in fact, answer their questions at a later time just as we said we would.

> Some parents use a double-standard, warning their daughters of sexual dangers while encouraging experimentation by their sons.[5]

If your kid never does come to you of his or her own volition with questions about sex, you will want to go ahead and initiate the discussions. Remember, it is our job as parents to reach out and take the lead in the discipleship process. Your child may blush and squirm initially, but that's OK. He or she needs to know that sex is something you two can talk about, not something shameful and secretive that need not be mentioned.

Here's another tip. Make sure you are aware of what programs your child's school plans to conduct about sex, and don't hesitate to deny your child's participation if you feel the prevailing message contradicts yours. I have vivid memories of a couple coming to speak at my middle school and teaching us how to put condoms on cucumbers. Their attitude was that we were all bound to start having sex as young people, so we needed to know how to use protection. I remember thinking, "I guess they're right. Everyone is doing it, so I'm sure I will too at some point." What a tragic thought to impress on a 12-year-old.

SINGLE PARENTS

If you are a single father raising a daughter or a single mother raising a son, that presents some unique challenges. While you can convey, to a great extent, wisdom and truth to your child about sex, you really need someone that is the same gender as your child to come alongside you and assist with communication. There are certain things about sex that a boy needs to hear from a man, and likewise, a girl needs to have a woman she can go to with her questions. If you don't have a relative who could help inspire abstinence in your child, perhaps there is someone in your church or community.

Small group formats can be a great outlet for this kind of ministry. For example, one or two adult men can meet with several young men, and as a group, they can discuss the issues surrounding sex. The important thing is that you find adults who have the spiritual maturity and integrity to be godly role models and who understand how to go about inspiring abstinence. **The Parent-Child Discussion Starter** questions provided in the Application Section make this book an ideal tool for conducting small groups with young people, especially when used in conjunction with the companion book for teens, *Why Wait? The Naked Truth About Sex and Abstinence.*

> **If older siblings are aggressive, sexually active, or drug users, younger siblings are more likely to follow their example than to learn from their mistakes.**[6]

Is It Time?

If you feel it's time to start having straightforward talks with your child about sex, you are ready to proceed to the second step of this study—Application. As we conclude the preparation section of the book, I encourage you to take some time to review and consider your answers to all of the previous **Questions for Thought** found at the end of each chapter and also respond to the questions below.

Questions for Thought:

1. Did your parents talk to you about sex? Was there anything about their approach you want to imitate? In what ways do you want to do things differently with your kids?

2. What are some benefits of praying with your child for his or her future mate?

3. Are you aware of what sex education programs your child's school plans to conduct? If not, how might you get informed?

4. What in this chapter stood out to you the most and why? What do you plan to do as a result?

5. What changes and/or adjustments have you made since reading the preparation section of this book?

SECOND STEP:

Application

Preparation

\+

Application

\+

Motivation

\=

Inspiration

I finally made up my mind that I was going to paint the wood paneling in my breakfast room. I got everything I needed for the job at the local hardware store, and as I pulled into the driveway, I was anxious to get started. I threw on my mismatched painting clothes, tied my hair back in a scrunchie, and popped the lid off the new can of white paint.

It suddenly dawned on me that I hadn't applied painter's tape to the floor and walls around the paneling. The thought of putting that lid back on, going back to the store for tape, and spending the next several hours taping off the room did not appeal to me in the least. I decided I would just be extra careful and not get paint any-where but on the wood—to heck with painters tape!

That was three months ago. Do you know what I did for four hours yesterday? Using a scrub brush and some heavy-duty sol-vent, I continued the process of scouring white blobs of paint off the ceramic tiles on my breakfast room floor. So much for not drip-ping. Oh, how I wish I had taken the time to prepare the room be-fore I started painting!

If changing wall colors requires prep work, how much more does something as significant as inspiring abstinence in our kids? Parents, I commend you for completing the Preparation section of this book! (You *did* complete it, right?) If you have taken the prin-ciples in the previous chapters to heart, you've done the necessary prep work in order to confidently proceed with the Application phase. You can be sure your efforts at instilling abstinence are not going to be half-hearted or sloppy, but rather, deliberate and effec-tive. (I wish I could say the same for my breakfast room paint job!)

From this point on, the book is designed to equip you to conduct engaging discussions with your child based on the material covered in each chapter. As you will see, I have provided **Parent-Child Discussion Starters**. The following tips will help you effectively utilize them:

☆ Read each chapter in its entirety *before* attempting to discuss it with your child. You may want to read the chapters several times if that's what it takes for you to feel confident explaining the information to your son or daughter.

☆ Each upcoming chapter has a corresponding chapter in the book for teens, "Why Wait?" As you will see, I have noted the specific corresponding chapter so that you and your child can each read beforehand and come to the discussion time "on the same page," so to speak.

☆ While it might be helpful to highlight certain sentences or paragraphs that you want to read to your child, you want to avoid reading entire chapters to him or her verbatim. Remember, this is a *discussion* with your child. Make a point to converse about the material versus launching into lengthy monologues.

☆ You may want to write down or type up the **Parent-Child Discussion Starter** questions so that your child can write down his or her answers, versus having to verbalize answers on the spot.

☆ You can give the **Parent-Child Discussion Starter** questions to your child a day or two in advance, or you may choose to provide them at the time of your discussion— just make sure you allow plenty of time for your child to think about and/or write responses.

☆ If your child does write down responses, explain that you are not going to take up his paper or look at his answers. It is simply an opportunity for him to record his own thoughts and opinions.

☆ Decide in advance where you will conduct your discussions. Choose places that are free from distractions. Avoid public settings where you and your child feel nearby strangers are overhearing your conversation.

☆ Don't pressure yourself do get through an entire chapter worth of material in one setting. Take all the time you and your child need.

☆ I believe you will find the **Discussion Roadmaps**, provided at the end of each chapter, very helpful as you discuss your child's answers. They help remind us of all the pertinent points we want to expound on.

OK, are you ready to get started? Take a deep breath. Go ahead and exhale. Now turn the page—by God's grace, *you can do this!*

SACRED

What's so Sacred About Sex?

Corresponds with Chapter Two "Why Wait?"

Today in my aerobics class, the instructor played a song that made me want to shout, "Stop the madness!" at the top of my lungs. The vocalist described in detail what sexual positions he wanted to try out on the object of his lust. He then sang a chorus that went something like, "everywhere we go, everybody knows, we're just animals."

Hollywood conveys this same message about human sexuality, as if we're all helpless victims of our sexual instincts and animalistic desires. Sex with anyone, anywhere, is not only accepted, but celebrated. Consequently, young people today view sex as a purely physical act that is about as sacred as an experience at the grocery store self check-out register. *No need for a personal connection— just give me what I came for, and I'll be on my way!*

Now let's not be so "spiritual" that we ignore that sex is, in fact, a physical act. It starts with physical attraction, leads to physical touch, and culminates with physical gratification. During sex, our bodies are flooded with hormones and endorphins that cause a chemical "high" of sorts. Obviously if sex didn't feel good, we would have no desire to do it.

But God help the society that sees sex as nothing *more* than physical! Throughout the world's historic account, once a nation lost all regard for the sacredness of sex and scoffed at sexual boundaries, it wasn't long before they found themselves suffering from hardship, famine, or complete annihilation. Pompeii is a great example. They were known for their infatuation with phallic symbols and statues, and they reveled in eroticism, that is, until the entire city was buried alive by lava in a single day.

The Book of Jude provides a biblical example that there are eventual consequences for widespread sexual deviance:

> *...as Sodom and Gomorrah, and the cities around them in a similar manner to these, having given themselves over to sexual immorality and gone after strange flesh, are set forth as an example, suffering the vengeance of eternal fire* (Jude 1:7).

Is it just me or does the phrase *"suffering the vengeance of eternal fire"* sound slightly serious? Obviously the infectious nature of perversion *is* serious! Now it's time to look at why …

SEX, A COVENANT RITUAL

It is difficult to grasp the concept of covenant in this day. We are a society of contracts, not covenants, and there is a *huge difference* between the two. We enter into contracts by signing on the dotted line and usually face financial consequences should we violate the terms of agreement. On the contrary, covenant rituals and commitments, as practiced by the ancient Israelites and portrayed in the Bible:

Covenant: A formal solemn agreement between two or more persons to do or not do something specified.

1. were sealed with blood,

2. created a "what's mine is yours and what's yours is mine" partnership,

3. demanded death for covenant violators, and

4. were witnessed by God.

The concept of covenants was invented by God, not humanity, and was created as a sacred, lifelong commitment between parties. Let's take a look at how God's plan for sex is clearly illustrated through these covenant rituals. In doing so, we will see the logical reasons that sex is a sacred and spiritual act.

1. Covenants are sealed with blood.

Historically, when two parties entered into covenant with each other, bloodshed was part of the covenant ceremony. Now please don't misunderstand me—no one was killed in the process! They either shed a light portion of their own blood or used blood from a dead animal.

You have probably realized by now that I like to ask *why*. That being said, I couldn't help but wonder why blood was God's chosen sealing agent for covenants. Why not wine, tears, or a firm handshake? After a considerable amount of thought, I believe it is because our blood is the tangible representation of our lives. Sealing a covenant in blood meant a person was giving *his life* to that partnership, not just his word or signature. With current technology, we now know that our genetic identity is in our blood. Thus to shed blood in a covenant ritual was to say, "I'm giving myself to you."

The wine is the token of God's new covenant to save you—an agreement sealed with the blood that Jesus poured out for you (see Luke 22:20).

How much do you know about God's covenant with Abraham? Please read Genesis 17 if you are unfamiliar with this historical event. When God entered into a covenant relationship with Abraham, He required that Abraham and all of his descendants be circumcised as a sign of the covenant. That certainly involved the shedding of blood. (I imagine there were some tears shed as well!) And what happened when Christ ushered in a new covenant? He sealed the covenant in His own blood, shed for you and me on the cross at Calvary.

Here's the point. *Marriage is a covenant commitment, and sex is the corresponding covenant ritual.* Read that last sentence as many times as you need to until you completely understand.

God designed sex to be the sealing act between a man and a woman who have entered into a lifelong commitment of marriage. Want proof of this? Well, we've already established that in order to enter into covenant, bloodshed is required. Now think about how the female body was created. When a woman has sex for the first time, the hymen is penetrated, which most often causes her to lightly bleed. Keep in mind, there is no biological function or identifiable purpose for the hymen—we just know that it is penetrated the first time a woman has intercourse and that it creates bloodshed. So you see, when a woman and a man save themselves for marriage and have sex on their wedding night, it is a covenant ritual sealing their partnership in blood! Isn't that just amazing?

God designed sex to be the sealing act between a man and a woman who have entered into a lifelong commitment of marriage.

Each time a couple makes love from that day on, it is a celebration and reminder of their covenant commitment. Isn't it just incredible to consider that children are created as a result of our covenant celebration with our mate? Life literally comes from the love and commitment we have with our spouse! (At least, according to the Bible, that is how God designed it to work.)

Now think about the tragedy of a young girl having her first sexual experience out of wedlock with an eager young man looking to "score," perhaps a backseat experience of some sort. What a waste of something profound! They have both robbed each other, and their future mates, by engaging in a covenant *ritual* without any covenant *commitment* with someone who is not even their covenant partner.

I like to ask young people, "Who is worthy to have this covenant sealing experience with you? That guy with the nice car, the giggly girl who sits at your lunch table?" They shake their heads no and admit that only their future spouse deserves to share that experience with them.

2. Covenant relationships create a "what's mine is yours and what's yours is mine" partnership.

Covenant terms can be summed up by saying, "What's mine is yours and what's yours is mine." This took on very literal meanings for the Israelites. When covenant partners needed financial help, they gave it. If their covenant partner went to war, they fought right beside him. Even after their covenant partner died, they took care of that person's descendants' needs when necessary.

This is how God intends marriage to be. In my marriage, my husband and I don't look at our finances in terms of what's his versus what's mine. Our finances are just that—*our* finances. We are a blended family, but my husband does not say to me, "That's *your* daughter." She's *our* daughter. When he is going through a difficult time, it's not his problem; it's *our* problem. That is the covenant partner mindset we work to maintain.

Those are all physical examples of the oneness that covenant brings, but the Bible tells us that there is a *spiritual* oneness as well. Consider this passage of Scripture, "Do you not know that he who is joined to [has sex with] a harlot is one body with her? For, 'the two,' He says, 'shall become one flesh'" (1 Cor. 6:16).

How is it that sex makes *two people one flesh?* You and I both know that we don't become physically joined together permanently after having sex with someone, yet that is what the above passage says. Can you imagine having sex with your spouse and waking up the next day to find you must live the rest of your lives as Siamese twins?

Actually, you may already realize that the "one flesh" existence that this passage of Scripture is speaking of takes place in the *spirit* realm. You see, when two people partake of the covenant ritual—sex—God sees them as one. They are still two people, but they have become one unified entity and partnership through a covenant relationship. After all, *oneness is the essence of covenant.* The spiritual connection that sex creates is a wonderful thing when we are married, but it is a tragedy when we are not, which is why the Bible warns against promiscuous sexual relationships. The "one flesh" union is meant to be shared with one person, unlike a harlot, who is joined to many partners.

STDs: A Spiritual Example

True or false: *STDs are the result of sex.* Most people don't hesitate to say true to this question, but that's not entirely correct. If STDs are the result of sex, how come two faithfully married people can have all the sex they want without any fear of catching an STD? In reality, STDs are the result of *illicit* sex—sex outside of God's intended boundaries (one partner for life).

One out of every two sexually active young people can expect to become infected with an STD by age 25.[1]

Furthermore, I believe sexually transmitted diseases are an outward sign of a spiritual reality, something we can see to warn us about what we *cannot* see. Think about how STDs work. Guy A gets an STD from his sexually infected partner, girl B. Then guy A infects girl C, who then infects guy D. Even though infected girl B and guy D have never even met, he will carry her STD.

And so it is in the spirit realm. We have all these covenant unions that connect us in unnatural ways to people we've never even met. Consider the following discovery.

> **The first "map" of teen sexual behavior has found a chain of 288 one-to-one sexual relationships at a high school in the U.S. Midwest, meaning that the teenager at the end of the chain may have had direct sexual contact with only one person, but indirect contact with 286 others.**[2]

Since covenant declares, "What's mine is yours, and what's yours is mine," what really happens when we're *spiritually* linked to a network of strangers? No wonder many sexually active singles complain of feeling depressed! Sex was designed by God to bond us intimately to one lifelong partner, but in premarital sexual activity, we find that we are just another soul added to a huge, oddly connected crowd of people we don't even know.

Are you aware that:

- ☆ Sexually active girls are more than *three times* more likely to be depressed than are girls who are not sexually active; sexually active boys are more than *twice as likely* to be depressed as are those who are not sexually active.[3]

- ☆ Sexually active girls are nearly *three times* more likely to attempt suicide than are girls who are not sexually active; sexually boys are *eight times* more likely to attempt suicide than are boys who are not sexually active.[4]

In summary, spiritual unions should not be taken lightly, which is why sex should not be taken lightly!

> **There are no marketed microbicides or vaccines (with the exception of the Hepatitis B vaccine) for the prevention of STDs.**[5]

3. Covenant requires death for those who forsake their commitment.

I'm glad cell phone companies and fitness centers use contracts instead of covenants, otherwise I'd be dead right now! That was a lighthearted comment, but in all seriousness, historically, those who broke the terms of their covenant commitments faced punishment by death. Knowing this, people did not enter into covenant lightly. They knew their very lives were at stake.

> **When surveyed, 53.2 percent of teens age 15-19 agree with the following statement, "It is alright for unmarried 18-year-olds to have sexual intercourse if they have strong affection for each other."[6]**

Now contrast this with our society's acceptance of sex outside of marriage. If breaking one's covenant terms was punishable by death, what must God think of two people who engage in a covenant *ritual* (sex) with no covenant *commitment* to begin with? In such cases, we are doing more than breaking the terms of covenant; we are trampling on the sacredness and necessity of covenant altogether.

Sex is supposed to be a bonding experience that uniquely connects us to our covenant partner. Furthermore, there is a direct correlation between casual sex and casual divorce. As our nation's premarital sex statistics go up, so does our divorce rate. Nearly one out of every two high school youths is sexually active, and nearly one out of every two marriages ends in divorce in our country.[7]

What happens to a post-it note that gets stuck and re-stuck to one surface after another? It loses its stickiness, at which point it no longer serves its purpose. And so it is with promiscuity. As our nation embraces the idea that sex with one partner after another is perfectly acceptable, there is no "sticking power" to sex. The only way the tides will change is if people like you and me teach our kids the truth about the sacredness of sex and the seriousness of the marriage covenant.

4. Covenants are witnessed by God.

Did you have a traditional wedding? If so, you probably invited lots of guests to witness the joyous occasion. Having all eyes on us while we say our marriage vows provides us with a small sense of what is truly taking place on a much larger scale in the spirit realm. Scripture makes it clear that God Himself is a witness to our covenant commitment.

> ...the Lord has been witness between you and the wife of your youth... (Malachi 2:14).

Earlier in First Corinthians 6:16, we read that two people who have sex become one flesh. In Matthew 19:5-6, we see that a husband and wife become one flesh:

> For this reason a man shall leave his father and mother and be joined to his wife, and the two shall become one flesh. So then, they are no longer two but one flesh. Therefore what God has joined together, let not man separate.

It is obvious in Scripture that sex and marriage are interconnected, and neither act is meant to be experienced without the other.

I would also like to point out that *God* joins a man and woman together, and He is a witness to our covenant commitment and ritual (see Malachi 2:14). Knowing this, I like to remind young people that when they join themselves to another through sexual behavior, whether married or not, they can be sure that *God is witnessing it.*

> Why did people in the Old Testament practice polygamy? For answers to this question and more, log on to www.InspiringAbstinence.com.

A DEEPER LOOK AT SEX

Growing up, I used to love to go to a certain store in the mall that had Magic Eye pictures. When I first glanced at one of the framed pieces of artwork, I thought, "Who in their right mind would buy this? It looks like a bunch of sloppy spaghetti noodles." But as I stood there and stared, something amazing happened. I suddenly saw a breathtaking 3-D image of an eagle soaring high above snow-capped mountains. I blinked a bit, and just as quickly as the beautiful artwork had appeared, I lost it again and saw only the messy spaghetti. I learned that there was a certain trick the lines play on your eyes and if you could focus just right, every ugly picture there actually concealed a gorgeous multiple layer image. Not everyone was patient enough to make their way around the store to try and see the hidden beauty masked on each canvas, but I loved to, simply because the images impressed me so much.

Sex can be the same way. At first glance, it looks like little more than a physical act. But if we're willing to focus on the Creator's real purpose for sex, we will see that it is a much deeper, richer experience than we originally imagined. God made sex to be an astounding gesture of love and commitment between two lifelong covenant partners. How sad that not everyone sees it this way. What a blessing that you and I can paint a different picture of sex for our kids!

Questions for Thought:

(Before discussing the material with your child):

1. How do you anticipate your child will respond to the **Parent-Child Discussion Starter** questions?

2. Where and when do you plan to meet?

3. What is the most vital concept in the chapter that you want your child to grasp? How do you plan to stress this point?

(After discussing the material with your child):

4. What went really well? What challenges did you have?

5. Is there anything you want to do differently during your next discussion?

Parent–Child Discussion Starters

For a reminder on how to use the Parent-Child Discussion Starters, please turn to page .

1. In your opinion, how does Hollywood (television and the media) portray sex? As something special? Dirty? Casual? Sacred?

2. Do you believe sex is merely a physical act or is there something more sacred to it? Why?

3. What do you think a *covenant* is?

4. You may or may not be aware that females experience light bloodshed the first time they have intercourse. In your opinion, why in the world did God create females' bodies to do this? Any ideas?

5. Put a check by the sentences that you believe are true:

   ❏ The Bible teaches that sex creates a spiritual bond.

   ❏ STDs are rare among young people.

   ❏ STDs are the result of sex.

   ❏ As the number of people having sex before marriage increases, so does our nation's divorce rate.

6. TRUE or FALSE: God is a witness when we get married and have sex with our spouse. _____

7. When the Bible talks about "two becoming one," it's referring to (check all that you agree with):

   ❏ two people who are married.

   ❏ two people who have had sex.

   ❏ I have no idea!

8. Do you believe sex outside of marriage is a sin? Why or why not?

Discussion Roadmap

For a reminder on how to use Discussion Roadmaps, please turn back to page 16.

1. **In your opinion, how does Hollywood (television and the media) portray sex? As something special? Dirty? Casual? Sacred?**

   a. Hollywood seriously misrepresents sexuality and the sacredness of sex (see page 99).

   b. Perhaps you and/or your child can think of some specific examples you have recently seen.

2. **Do you believe sex is simply a physical act or is there something more sacred to it than that? Why?**

   a. Sex is a physical act but has spiritual implications (see page 48).

3. **What do you think a covenant is?**

   a. *Covenant:* A formal solemn agreement between two or more persons to do or not do something specified (see page 100).

   b. Covenant rituals and commitments, as practiced by the ancient Israelites and portrayed in the Bible (explain each of the following points; feel free to read certain portions of the chapter text if need be):

   ☆ Were sealed with blood.

   ☆ Entitled covenant partners to each other's goods, resources, and support.

   ☆ Demanded death for covenant violators.

   ☆ Were witnessed by God (see page 101).

c. The concept of covenants was invented by God, not humankind, and was created as a sacred, lifelong commitment between parties (see page 103).

4. **You may or may not be aware that females experience light bloodshed the first time they have intercourse. In your opinion, why in the world did God create females' bodies to do this? Any ideas?**

a. Covenants required bloodshed (Abraham, Christ) (see page 101).

b. When a woman has sex for the first time, the hymen is penetrated, which causes her to lightly bleed (see page 102).

c. God designed sex to be the sealing act between a man and a woman who have entered into a lifelong commitment of marriage (see page 102).

d. Marriage is a covenant commitment and sex is the corresponding covenant ritual (see page 103).

e. Who is worthy to have this covenant-sealing experience with you (see page 103)?

5. **Put a check by the sentences that you believe are true:**

❏ The Bible teaches that sex creates a spiritual bond.

a. Covenant terms can be summed up by saying, "What's mine is yours and what's yours is mine" (see page 103).

b. "Do you not know that he who is joined to [has sex with] a harlot is one body with her? For, 'the two,' He says, 'shall become one flesh,'" (1 Cor. 6:16).

c. The "one flesh" existence that this passage of Scripture is speaking of takes place in the spirit realm— we don't become Siamese twins (see page 104).

    d. Read the paragraph about what researchers discovered when they "mapped" the sexual link between students at a particular high school (see page 105).

❑ **STDs are rare among young people.**

    e. One in every two sexually active young people catches an STD by 25 years of age (see page 104).

❑ **STDs are the result of sex.**

    f. Not entirely true! STDs are the result of illicit sex; sex outside of God's intended boundaries (two faithfully married partners) (see page 104).

    h. Reference statistics regarding depression and suicide among sexually active teens (see page 105).

❑ **As the number of people having sex before marriage increases, so does our nation's divorce rate.**

    i. If breaking one's covenant terms was punishable by death, what must God think of two people who engage in a covenant *ritual* (sex) with no covenant *commitment* to begin with (see page 106)?

    j. One out of every two high school youths is sexually active and one out of every two marriages ends in divorce in our country (see page 106).

    k. Share sticky-note analogy (see page 106).

6. **TRUE or FALSE: God is a witness when we get married and have sex with our spouse.**

    True; "...the Lord has been a witness between you and the wife of your youth" (Malachi 2:14).

7. **When the Bible talks about "two becoming one," it's referring to (check all that you agree with):**

    ❑ two people who are married.

    ❑ Yes, Matthew 19:5-6.

❏ two people who have had sex.

❏ Yes, First Corinthians 6:16.

❏ It is obvious in Scripture that sex and marriage are interconnected, and neither act is meant to be experienced without the other (see page 107).

❏ When we join ourselves to another through sexual behavior, whether married or not, we can be sure that God is witnessing it (see page 108).

❏ **I have no idea!**

That's okay. Just share the points mentioned above.

8. **Do you believe sex outside of marriage is a sin? Why or why not?**

❏ This is a topic we will explore during our next discussion together.

In Summary

☆ Share the Magic Eye picture illustration (see page 108).

☆ Discuss the statements and statistics that are highlighted in boxes throughout the chapter.

☆ Ask your child, "Do you have any questions about what we've discussed today?"

8

SIN

Why Is Premarital Sex a Sin?

Corresponds with Chapter Three in "Why Wait?"

It is clear throughout the Scriptures that sex outside of marriage, referred to as fornication, is a sin (an offensive act in God's sight), *but why?*

But fornication...let it not even be named among you (Ephesians 5:3).

If the only thing we have told our children about abstinence is that premarital sex is a sin, we are right, but in *serious* need of more information. The nature of temptation is to exploit our children's lack of knowledge and to make them question the validity of God's standards. Should our kids find themselves in the throes of temptation, these kinds of thoughts will bombard their minds:

☆ *What's the big deal?*

☆ *One night of pleasure isn't going to hurt anyone.*

☆ *If sex is so bad, why does it feel so good?*

☆ *What difference would a band on my ring finger really make?*

Believing that premarital sex is a sin is one thing; knowing *why* is another. Once kids know *why*, they are far better equipped to quench the "fiery darts" of temptation—the thoughts that attempt to sway them.

EXPLAINING SIN TO KIDS

Young people tend to let out a sigh of relief when I inform them that sex is *not* a sin. It was invented by God and is intended to bring pleasure, intimacy, and precious new lives into being. The sighs are replaced by puzzled faces, however, when I explain, "Sex only *becomes* a sin when we disregard God's boundaries and lose sight of the sacredness of sex." They immediately want to know what in the world I mean when I say that sex can become sinful. They also want a clear explanation for these so-called boundaries God has placed on sex.

Before we can fully answer the question posed in this chapter's title, "Why is premarital sex considered sinful," our kids have to understand what sin is. Do you know there's a difference between *sins* and *sin*? We can all think of examples of *sins* (plural)—lying, stealing, murdering, cheating—you get the point. But what about *sin* (singular)? In the Bible, *sin* refers to the nature inside of us all that wants to commit sins. Furthermore, this *sin nature* can be summarized in one word—**self-centeredness**. Add your own examples of *sins* to the few I previously mentioned and you will see that all of them, without fail, are rooted in self-centeredness. Self-centeredness grieves God because it is totally contrary to His loving, giving nature.

When we talk to kids about sex before marriage being a sin, it goes a long way to show them how it is a self-centered act, a concept that they are apt to comprehend. To do this, we must show them the difference between *love* and *lust*.

LOVE VERSUS LUST

Consider the following contrasting attributes:

LOVE	LUST
Desires to satisfy another at the expense of self.	Desires to satisfy self at the expense of another.
Is easily satisfied.	Is never satisfied.
Has nothing to hide.	Often operates in secret.
Brings peace.	Brings guilt.
Is open and honest.	Manipulates and disguises intentions.
Is concerned for another's wellbeing.	Is consumed with selfish desires.
Remains faithful during tough times.	Abandons when needs are not met.
Sees all that is beautiful about a person.	Has eyes fixed strictly on outward beauty.
Is patient.	Is impatient.

According to some research, lust and affection arise from different parts of the brain.[1]

When it comes to sex, a person is either operating in love or lust. We can't operate in both simultaneously because they are diametrically opposed. God's plan for sex is based on love, not lust. Why is premarital sex sinful? In a single sentence, *because it is the result of lust,* which we know is rooted in self-centeredness and is, therefore, sinful.

Love is patient and kind. Love is not jealous or boastful or proud or rude. [Love] does not demand its own way. It is not irritable and it keeps no record of being wronged. It [is never glad] about injustice but rejoices whenever the truth wins out. Love never gives up, never loses faith, is always hopeful, and endures through every circumstance (1 Corinthians 13:4-7 NLT).

Sex is a covenant celebration reserved for our covenant partner. To have sex with someone who is not our mate is to take something from them that does not belong to us. It is to put our immediate physical desires above their long-term spiritual blessings (and ours as well). We also shortchange our future mate, who is the only person deserving of the gift of our virginity. Sex before marriage often involves manipulation, secrecy (hiding from parents), infatuation with outward appearances, and impatience, all of which are indicative of lust.

A great exercise to do with young people is to have them write down the benefits of having sex before marriage and the benefits of waiting until marriage. The only benefit they usually come up with for premarital sex is the liberty to have sex without the wait. Since love is patient, we know that this is a lustful, self-centered motive, which means it is rooted in sin.

Percent of all teens 15-17 who agree with the following statements about the benefits of waiting to have sex:[2]

Respect for yourself	93%
Stay in control of your relationship	91%
Respect from parents	91%
Keeping true to religious values	91%

Respect from friends		84%
No worry of pregnancy or STDs		79%
One less thing to worry about		78%

THE LOVE TEST—WILL HE WAIT?

Some dear friends of mine reared their child based on the principles of inspired abstinence. Now that their daughter is grown and married, she has some very important things to say about the issue of love versus lust (she prefers to stay anonymous). Her comments are directed at young ladies, but the same principles can certainly be applied to young men. Keep in mind, when she uses the word *courtship*, she's referring to the time leading up to marriage where a couple is bonding and preparing for a lifetime together:

Two-thirds of U.S. teenagers who have had sexual relations wish they had waited longer.[3]

While dating, we may consider it a sign of love that our boyfriend wants to have sex with us or go too far. He thinks we're beautiful, sexy, and wonderful. But after marriage, his constant desire for sex can become a painful source of aggravation. The emotions that were so charming and amorous during courtship seem to get between the love we want to feel and the fact that men crave sex so intensely. It might be flattering at first, but what about the nights we would rather go to sleep? We have had a bad day and feel cranky, and suddenly find ourselves yelling, "It's always been about sex with you, hasn't it?" We wonder, "Would he love me if I didn't have sex with him?" If this question isn't answered before marriage, it is so hard after marriage to believe our husband sincerely loves us for who we are on the inside, for more than our physical "usefulness." Don't we all want to know deep in our hearts in a way that gives real security that we are loved for who we really are?

Our husband is meant to be our protector from the world, but if in courtship, he takes a part of us sexually, with no regard to the cost, our trust is already violated. We're left thinking, "He said he'd do anything for me, but that obviously didn't include controlling his sexual desires until we were married." Wait a minute! There are many scenarios in life where we really want our husband to take the responsibility to control himself. Do you want him to take out the trash without glaring at you or complaining? Watch the kids so you can shop for groceries in peace for an hour? Resist a seductive co-worker?

Courtship is meant to be a time of laying the foundation of trust, which is facilitated by a man choosing to honor the woman he loves, *putting her worth above his own desires*. Abstaining from sex before marriage goes a long way toward settling the issue that we are truly *loved* by a man, as opposed to merely lusted after. If he has the love of Christ, he will have constraint ("The love of Christ constrains us," (see 2 Cor. 5:14)).

SEXUAL BOUNDARIES

When used correctly, condoms are highly effective against the spread of HIV. Condoms have "low effectiveness," however, against the spread of Herpes, Syphilis, Chancroid, and HPV.[4]

One way to explain to our kids God's boundaries for sex is to use the example of a river. A river is a beautiful flowing body of water, ideal for recreation and relaxation. But what happens when a river rages beyond the boundaries of its banks? It becomes a destructive flood, damaging and destroying everything in its path! And so it is with sex. Within the boundaries of marriage, it is safe and enjoyable, but outside of marriage, it becomes a destructive act. When young people are asked to write down all the potential consequences of premarital sex they can think of, and we discuss their list with them, the beauty of God's boundary of marriage becomes obvious.

Marriage is honorable among all, and the bed undefiled; but fornicators and adulterers God will judge (Hebrews 13:4).

God sets boundaries for the same reason that we do as parents—for the protection and well-being of His children. My 4-year-old daughter called me, "the worst mommy ever," one day because I wouldn't let her have another cookie. She was fighting off a cold, and I didn't want her immune system compromised by eating too many sweets. I wanted her to recover and be healthy. Since I had the audacity to stand between her and her desire, I became the enemy.

Every day 8,000 teenagers become infected by an STD.[5]

Sometimes we're guilty of making God out to be the one standing between us and the pleasure we feel we deserve. Young people, in particular, tend to erroneously envision God peering down from Heaven with a lightning bolt aimed at their heads, just waiting to release it the minute they start having fun. How untrue that is! On the contrary, *all God is trying to do is get good things* **to** *our kids and keep bad stuff* **away** *from them!* When God says sex is reserved for marriage, it's because He's trying to protect them, not prevent them from experiencing pleasure.

Just think about this. If all of the world's children today waited until they were married to have sex and then stayed faithful to their spouses, STDs would be eradicated in a single generation! STDs are a curse that operate in the earth because humankind is not doing things God's way. God is not putting disease on people; we welcome disease when we push past the protective barriers that God has established.

Darkness results when no light is present. And so it is with God. He's not the Creator of life's tragedies; they are the curse on this earth because humankind, as a whole, has rejected God and His light (His Son). And how dark sexual acts can become when God's purposes are rejected! Tragedies like rape, incest, molestation, and prostitution are all the end result of using the God-given gift of sex in ways that He never designed it to be used. Even though we tend to think of fornication as less offensive than those acts, it is equally outside the purpose of God's plan, and engaging in it is a rejection of God's instructions.

SEXUAL IMMORALITY, A UNIQUE SIN

First Corinthians 6:18-20 say:

Flee sexual immorality. Every sin that a man does is outside the body, but he who commits sexual immorality sins against his own body. Or do you not know that your body is the temple of the Holy Spirit who is in you, whom you have from God, and you are not your own? For you were bought at a price; therefore glorify God in your body and in your spirit, which are God's.

I used to wonder what that passage meant when it said that sexual immorality is a sin against our own bodies. After prayer and consideration, I now have an idea what it means. Sin often involves an instrument of sin. For example, for a drug dealer, it's drugs. For a materialistic woman, it's money. For a murderer, it's a weapon. But when we engage in fornication, our *bodies* become the instrument of sin. The reason this is so offensive is because the Holy Spirit dwells in us!

Here is a great example that I've used over the years to help young people grasp this concept. I ask them what they would think if I told them that a gang of young men broke into the neighborhood donut shop and vandalized it. They painted the walls, broke chairs, shattered glass, and ruined the place. The young people respond that they would think that was awful. Then I ask them what they would think if I told them that a gang of young men vandalized a local *church.* They broke in, ripped up the pews, painted obscene pictures on the pulpit, tore pages out of Bibles, and totally trashed the place. Wide-eyed, they respond, "That would be horrible, way worse than the donut shop!" That's the perfect time to explain that the presence of God does not live in buildings, not even in church sanctuaries. He lives in us! We are the Church! So you see, to enter into sexual sin with our bodies is to "trash the temple," and that is a wicked act.

Ninety-three percent of teenagers believe that teens should be given a strong message from society to abstain from sex.[6]

A POLITICALLY INCORRECT WORD

If there is one word humanity doesn't like to hear, it's *sin.* Overly ambitious ministers, whose hearts are set on attaining huge congregations, often remove this word from their vocabulary altogether, knowing that it has the potential to offend and cause certain people to leave the pews. The problem is that the Gospel demands that we acknowledge our sin. It is only when we recognize our sinfulness, realize how offensive it is to God, and acknowledge how helpless we are to overcome sin by ourselves that we become aware of our desperate need for a Savior and call upon Jesus Christ.

There are those who suggest that it is unloving to use an ugly word such as *sin.* While I do agree that it is an ugly word, I take serious offense to the notion that it is unkind to talk to people about it. As a matter of fact, the *only* loving thing to do is tell people the truth about sin, if given the opportunity. When followed by the good news of salvation through Christ, a discussion about sin is quite literally the most loving message we could ever tell anyone!

Mom or Dad, don't be afraid to use the word sin with your kids. While I strongly warn against instilling abstinence based solely on the notion that premarital sex is a sin, I implore you to avoid running into the other ditch where we downplay the seriousness of sin. If you wonder how serious sin is, look no further than the utter brutality of the cross. Jesus was beaten beyond recognition and died an excruciating death *because of our sin.*

Fornication is sinful, and our kids need to understand this. Based on the content of this chapter, let's do our best to explain *why.* Let's also help them understand that they will give account to God for the decisions that they make in this life, as will we. And while born-again Christians need not fear hell, since we are assured an eternity in Heaven based on Christ's sacrifice, we must acknowledge His Lordship in our lives by heeding His commandments. *While we in no way earn salvation through a sexually pure lifestyle, our obedience in that area is evidence that we have, in fact, bowed our knee to Christ's Lordship, which is a prerequisite for salvation.* (That's another one of those key statements that you might want to read repeatedly until it really sinks in.)

Proverbs 1:7 tells us, "The fear of the Lord is the beginning of knowledge." Parents, are we raising our kids to fear the Lord? That doesn't mean that we frighten them so that they shrink away from God in intimidation. It means that we teach them to respect and revere God and His commandments. Until our kids have a healthy fear and respect for God, they will not retain godly knowledge and values, which are essential for inspired abstinence.

...And by the fear of the Lord one departs from evil (Proverbs 16:6).

How do we instill these attributes in them? We model a lifestyle of loving what God loves and rejecting what God rejects. If you're not sure what God loves and what He rejects, that just means you need to get to know Him better. The more you get to know someone, like a spouse for example, the more aware you become of what they stand for and what they are repulsed by. Out of respect for those we love, we support what they value and avoid those things that they find offensive—it's no different with God. He gave us the

Bible and Jesus Christ's living example so that we could understand His nature. There are certain things about this world and humanity that God adores and other things He abhors. *To indulge ourselves in something God despises or to disregard something God highly esteems indicates that we lack a healthy fear of God.*

THE TRUE PURPOSE OF GRACE

Our kids need a proper understanding of grace and its purpose in their lives. There's a false message circulating in the Church today that erroneously assures people that sin is no longer an issue since we live under the dispensation of grace (the era after Christ's death). Many professing Christians live as if there is currently no moral law. "That was in the Old Testament," they say in a drunken state with a beer in one hand and a pornographic magazine in the other. It's true that we are no longer under the Old Testament law in terms of the rituals and regulations, but God's moral standards haven't changed a bit. Remember, Jesus said He came to *fulfill* the law, not *destroy* it.

> Jesus said: "Don't misunderstand why I have come. I did not come to abolish the law of Moses or the writings of the prophets. No, I came to accomplish their purpose" (Matthew 5:17 NLT).

I will attempt to correctly explain grace in a single sentence: *Grace does not make sin less sinful; it makes overcoming sin possible.* Go ahead, read it again.

> ...My Grace is sufficient for you, My strength is made perfect in [your] weakness... (2 Corinthians 12:9).

You and I do not have the ability to quit sinning by shear will power or self reliance, but when we lean on the leadership of the Holy Spirit (God's grace at work in our lives), we can find victory over old habits, addictions, and destructive patterns that have enslaved us for years. This not only glorifies God but also greatly benefits us!

So you see, grace does not mean that God no longer takes offense to sins, like fornication for example; it means that we have access to the spiritual strength that we need to resist and overcome temptation.

Speaking of temptation, our kids need to know that it is *not* a sin to be tempted. Sin occurs when we *yield* to temptation. If they don't understand this, they will be too ashamed to call on God when, in reality, they need Him the most! Should they find themselves under strong sexual temptation, they need not shy away from God, but on the contrary, aggressively run to Him for help.

How do we get God's help? *Ask and obey.* Admit that we need His intervention and then obey what He leads us to do. The Bible promises that God will always make a way of escape from temptation (see 1 Cor. 10:13). The problem is that we don't always walk through the door of escape that He provides.

I like to ask young people, "If you were on a diet, which would be the best place to go study, the library or an ice cream parlor?" They understand that it's foolish to sit in an ice cream shop while trying to avoid eating sweets. I then ask, "So if you've decided not to have sex with your boyfriend, where is the best place to hang out with him—a mall full of people or his house while his parents are gone?" This illustration helps kids understand that it is not wise to intentionally subject themselves to tempting situations and then complain that the temptation is too strong to resist. The way of escape requires using good judgment and avoiding tempting situations altogether when possible.

In Summary

Conveying the beauty of sex and the value of virginity to our kids is the emphasis of the next chapter. In the meantime, I applaud you for following through on your commitment to read this book. You have already made it halfway through the study!

Questions for Thought:

(Before discussing the material with your child)

1. Why is important that kids, first and foremost, know that premarital sex is sinful, and *why* is it sinful?

2. How does the provided explanation of grace compare with your original understanding of grace?

3. What is the most vital concept in the chapter that you want your child to grasp? How do you plan to stress this point?

(After discussing the material with your child):

4. What went really well? What challenges did you have?

5. What did your child seem to enjoy the most about this discussion?

Parent-Child Discussion Starters

1. How would you define the word *sin*?

2. In your opinion, what's the difference between loving and lusting after a member of the opposite sex?

3. What are some benefits of having sex before marriage? What are some benefits of waiting until you're married to have sex?

4. If your friend did not want to have sex until marriage but was dating someone who refused to wait... (check all that you agree with):

   ❑ You would encourage your friend to end the relationship

   ❑ You would doubt if that person really loves your friend

   ❑ You would tell your friend to go ahead and have sex with the person

5. Why do you think God commands His people to keep certain boundaries (i.e. no sex outside of marriage)?

6. What do you think the Bible means when it says, "He who commits sexual immorality sins against his own body" (1 Cor. 6:18)?

7. What do you think it means to fear God?

8. TRUE or FALSE: To live by grace means that sin is no longer an issue and that I can live however I want.

   _____

9. Do you think it's a sin to be tempted to do something you know you shouldn't? Why or why not?

10. Being a virgin is… (check all that you agree with):

❑ embarrassing if you're a young adult.

❑ something to be valued.

❑ not fun.

Discussion Roadmap

1. **How would you define the word *sin*?**

   a. Sex outside of marriage, known as fornication, is a sin—Ephesians 5:3 (see page 115).

   b. It's important that you know why fornication is considered sinful so that you can overcome the thoughts that undermine abstinence (see page 116).

   c. Explain the difference between *sin* and *sins* (see page 116).

   d. Our *sin nature* can be summarized in one word— *self-centeredness* (see page 116).

   e. Have a young person name some sins; ask, "How are they rooted in self-centeredness?"

2. **In your opinion, what's the difference between loving and lusting after a member of the opposite sex?**

   a. Review contrasting attributes of love versus lust (see page 117).

   b. God's plan for sex is based on love, not lust—can't operate in both (see page 117).

   c. Why is premarital sex sinful? In a single sentence, *because it is the result of lust,* which we know is rooted in self-centeredness and is, therefore, sinful (see page 118).

   d. To have sex with someone who is not our mate is to take something from them that does not belong to us (see page 118).

3. **What are some benefits of having sex before marriage? What are some benefits of waiting until you're married to have sex?**

   a. Discuss your child's answers.

   b. One of the only benefits of premarital sex is the liberty to have sex without the wait. Since love is patient, we know that this is a lustful, self-centered motive, which means that it is rooted in sin (see page 118).

   c. Read the text from the section "The Love Test—**Will He Wait?" (See page 119.)**

4. **If your friend did not want to have sex until marriage but was dating someone who refused to wait... (check all that you agree with):**

   ❑ **I would encourage my friend to end the relationship.**

   a. If checked, encourage your child to explain why they checked this statement and discuss the validity of his or her response.

   b. If not checked, ask why and explain that we would not want to date anyone who is operating in lust due to the attributes of lust.

   ❑ **I would doubt that person really loved my friend**

   c. Whether checked or not checked, reiterate that a person cannot operate in lust and love at the same time and that impatience is indicative of lust.

   ❑ **I would tell my friend to go ahead and have sex with the person.**

   d. If checked, ask why. Continue to reiterate concepts from last chapter and carefully communicate principles from the following chapters.

5 **Why do you think God commands His people to keep certain boundaries (i.e. no sex outside of marriage)?**

   a. Explain river illustration (see page 120).

   b. God sets boundaries for the same reason that we do as parents—for the protection and well-being of His children (see page 121).

    c. Ask, "Do you think God is trying to ruin your fun?" Explain: *all God is trying **to** do is get good things to you and keep bad stuff **away** from you!* When God says sex is reserved for marriage, it's because He's trying to protect you, not prevent you from experiencing pleasure (see page 121).

    d. STD's example: eradicate STDs if one generation would wait to have sex and stay married to their mates (see page 121).

6. **What do you think the Bible means when it says, "He who commits sexual immorality sins against his own body" (1 Cor. 6:18)?**

    a Explain instruments of sin; in fornication, our bodies are the instruments of sin (see page 122).

    b. Use the donut shop versus church vandalism exercise (see page 122).

    c. Explain that you are not going to apologize for using the word sin and that it is a necessary word to use (see page 123).

    d. Explain: while we in no way earn salvation through a sexually pure lifestyle, our obedience in that area is evidence that we have, in fact, bowed our knee to Christ's Lordship, which is a prerequisite for salvation (see page 124).

7. **What do you think it means to fear God?**

    a. "The fear of the Lord is the beginning of knowledge" (Prov. 1:7).

    b. To fear God is *not to* shrink away from him in terror but rather to revere (respect) Him and His commandments (see page 124).

    c. The practical way we fear God is by loving what God loves and rejecting what God rejects (see page 124).

    d. If we're not sure what God loves and what He rejects, that just means we need to get to know Him better—spouse illustration (see page 124).

8. **TRUE or FALSE: To live by grace means that sin is no longer an issue and that I can live however I want.**

    a. False: *grace does not make sin less sinful; it makes overcoming sin possible* (see page 125).

    b. Grace does not mean that God no longer takes offense to sins, like fornication for example; it means that we have access to the spiritual strength that we need to resist and overcome temptation (see page 125).

9. **Do you think it's a sin to be tempted to do something you know you shouldn't? Why or why not?**

    a. It is *not* a sin to be tempted. Sin occurs when we *yield* to temptation (see page 126).

    b. Don't be afraid or ashamed to call on God when you are suffering temptation (see page 126).

    c. How do we get God's help? Ask and obey (see page 126).

    d. The way of escape requires using good judgment and avoiding tempting situations altogether when possible—use studying at library versus ice cream parlor illustration (see page 126).

10. **Being a virgin is…(check all that you agree with):**

❑ embarrassing if you're a young adult.

❑ something to be valued.

❑ not fun.

❏ No need to discuss answers now; explain that this will be the topic of your next discussion.

IN SUMMARY

☆ Discuss the statements and statistics that are highlighted in boxes throughout the chapter.

☆ Ask your child, "Do you have any questions about what we've discussed today?"

VIRGINITY

How to Convey the Value of Virginity

Corresponds with Chapter Four in "Why Wait?"

God's answer to the young person who asks, "Can I have sex?" isn't, "No." It's simply, "Wait." Unlike the forbidden fruit in the Garden of Eden, which was *never* to be eaten, sex is different; we can freely partake of it *at the right time.*

There are two kinds of waiting: *enduring* and *anticipating.* When I have a basketful of groceries, a fussy toddler pulling at my pant leg, and five shoppers ahead of me in the checkout line, I begrudgingly *endure* the wait. But when I have something nice in layaway, on the other hand, waiting to bring home my merchandise is an exciting time of anticipation! Waiting is either a miserable chore or an eager time of expectancy depending on what we're waiting for. When there's something valuable and special coming our way, we consider the wait worthwhile.

Abstaining from sex is an absolute drag for the young person who doesn't understand the blessing that God has in store for his or her future. Inspired abstinence means that our kids do more than endure being virgins; they anticipate a meaningful reward for their patience. This is made possible when our kids understand what virginity is really about and how God intends to pour out blessings on their love life in the future.

JESSICA: POPULAR OR PREY?

I have a friend who has a husband who has a brother who has a daughter who is really in over her head! This attractive young lady started having sex in high school—and didn't stop. She sleeps with one guy after another and admits to having sex with six different guys just last month. Get this—she says these guys she's going to bed with are her *friends*.

This girl, whom we'll call Jessica, is quite popular among her peer group and is really enjoying all of the attention she's been getting since she started making herself "available" to the guys. It breaks my heart to think that she is too naive to understand what's really going on. She's being passed from one "friend" to the next so that they can use her and then hand her off to another eager young man looking to temporarily satisfy himself sexually. In reality, she's not popular; *she's prey*. And those guys don't really *like* her; they just *lust* after her.

Jessica really needs to understand the Coke can principle, and our kids do too!

THE COKE CAN PRINCIPLE

Tim comes inside after playing basketball with his friends and heads straight for the fridge. He swings open the door, takes a deep breath as the frosty air swarms around his sweaty face, and then grabs an ice cold can of Coke off the shelf. His desert-dry mouth begins to salivate as he pops the tab and pulls the can to his parched lips. What a refreshing sip! What a liberating burp!

Along comes James. "Hey Tim, give me a sip!" James takes a few gulps and then passes the Coke to William. William takes one large sip and then hands the can off to Peter. The coke is half empty, so Peter takes a small sip before passing it to Dillon. Dillon takes a few swigs but doesn't like the idea of drinking the last few sips. The Coke is now lukewarm and full of backwash. Dillon walks up to Tim, who took the Coke out of the fridge in the first place, and asks, "You want your Coke back Tim?"

"No way, dude! Not after everyone took a turn drinking out of it! I'll just get a new one out of the fridge."

Do you see why Jessica needs to understand the Coke can principle? HINT: Jessica *is* the Coke can!

Typical guys have an unspoken rule; *sleep with the easy girls; marry the virgin.* In other words, when guys are young and eager to play the field, they tend to ignore the "virginal" girls and flock to the females who are willing to have sex. However, when they mature and desire to find a wife and settle down, their attention turns from the "wild child" who has been passed around; instead, they seek a more modest woman to marry and be the mother of their children. It's not right, but it's the truth.

Virginity: More Than a Sexual Issue

The essence of virginity is *monogamy*—not just one partner for a season at a time, but one partner for *all* time. Furthermore, virginity is more than a physical state; it is a mindset. To have a virgin state of mind is to live with the belief that there is *one* person for you and that you are waiting for that special one.

The Lord directs the steps of the godly. He delights in every detail of their lives (Psalm 37:23 NLT).

When it comes to our kids, we all know that there is probably a myriad of attractive members of the opposite sex whose personalities would blend well with our kids' preferences someday when they are ready for marriage. However, there is only one whom God has picked to be their mate. Surely if God has promised to order our kids' steps and direct their paths (see Prov. 3:6), He has a mate in mind for them. Whom we choose to marry affects nearly every aspect of our lives! Once two people are joined in matrimony, they are integrated into one partnership "as long as they both shall live." That being said, God cannot plan our children's futures without planning the selection of their future mates.

That doesn't mean that our kids *have* to marry the one God has in mind for them. They have freewill and can pursue a relationship with whomever they choose. But following our own plan at the expense of seeking God's will for our lives always ends in disappointment, if not devastation. It is true that, by His loving grace, God can pick up the pieces of our poor decisions once we acknowledge that we've missed the mark, and He can even cause good to come from a less than ideal predicament. However, it's usually a difficult journey to "right the wrong," and we are not exempt from the consequences that our wayward actions have evoked. When it comes to something as significant as marriage, it is wise to seek God's Plan "A" for our lives (more about how to find the right mate in Chapter Fifteen).

What if it's not God's will that I get married someday? Log onto InspiredAbstinence.com for answers to this question and more.

Can you think of a time when you did things *your* way instead of God's way and paid a costly price for it? Why not tell that story to your son or daughter? Sharing personal testimonies with our kids is beneficial because it allows them to understand how God's principles work in everyday life without having to go through some of the hardships we did.

GOD: AN OUT-OF-TOUCH OLD MAN OR A HOPELESS ROMANTIC?

Young people tend to erroneously envision God as an elderly man with a long white beard sitting hunched over on a tacky gold throne floating around somewhere in outer space. They wonder how a being living in a heavenly realm can possibly identify with the butterflies and goose bumps that accompany human attraction. They can't imagine that God knows what it's like to feel "turned on" by the opposite sex or that He understands how the human heart races during a passionate kiss. The ironic thing is that God alone created sex, along with the fantastic physical reactions human sexuality brings.

This High Priest of ours understands our weaknesses, for He faced all of the same [temptations] we do, yet He did not sin (Hebrews 4:15 NLT).

Our kids need to be reminded that God knows exactly what it's like to be a human, not just because He created us and is all-knowing, but because He lived as a human in the person of Jesus Christ. Wrapping our minds around the Trinity (God existing simultaneously yet distinctly as the Father, the Son, and the Holy Spirit) is enough to give anyone a brain freeze, but we know by Jesus' own testimony that He was more than a man—*He was God living as a man.* That being said, Jesus must have experienced physical attraction during the 33 years He spent on earth. We know He was tempted sexually because the Bible says that He was tempted in every way a person can be, and yet did not give in (see Heb. 4:15).

The Bible shows us how in-touch God is with the intensity of human experiences, including our sexuality. While those who have never read the Bible may assume it's a conservative book full of child-friendly stories, nothing could be further from the truth. Sure, there are stories suitable for children, but the Bible is also packed full of detailed accounts of bloody battles, wicked villains, heroic warriors, and explicit sexual experiences. There's an entire book of the Bible, Song of Solomon, written in symbolism so that the adult content and blatant sexuality is cloaked in modesty. If you think that book is all about fruits and gardening, you might want to read it more carefully! It's a detailed account of passionate love-making and the wonder of human attraction. It also helps us understand the intensity with which God pursues and draws us to Him.

Parents, our kids need to know that God is romantic in nature and that He understands their sexual longings. Furthermore, His call to premarital virginity is all about romance! Which sounds more appealing:

☆ Two people "trying out" one person after another physically and emotionally until they finally find the one they think is the best?

☆ Two people saving their hearts and bodies for that one person who is to be their partner for life?

More than a quarter of 15 to 17-year-old girls say that sexual intercourse is "almost always" or "most of the time" part of a "casual relationship."[1]

God is writing a brilliant love story for our children, and if they will trust in His ability to provide the right mate at the right time, He will! It is our job, parents, to remind our kids that God has something special in store for their love life, something worth waiting for. We need to encourage our children about this on a regular basis because the hope of one partner for one lifetime is constantly being challenged by worldly influences.

THE PURPOSE OF SEX

Over the years, I've encouraged my kids to do everything they do with a purpose in mind. Whether that purpose is to advance God's Kingdom, prepare for the future, or just have a wonderful time with friends, I want my kids to make their decisions based on more than sheer emotion or peer pressure.

When it comes to sexual activity, the purpose is to produce a unique bond between two covenant partners. The resulting bond can be as tangible as creating a child together or as abstract as lingering feelings of attachment that resonate in our souls.

Sex and commitment may be intertwined by nature. Human physiological responses affect neurological patterns...As one scientist explains, those who engage in casual sex can trigger the brain system for attachment (as well as for romantic love), leading to complex, unanticipated emotional entanglement with psychologically and socially unsuitable mating partners.[2]

Did you know that certain chemical reactions take place in our brains during sex that actually cause a sort of *imprinting* to occur, meaning that the images of our sexual experiences are stored in our minds with heightened detail and permanence? Just like certain animals have chemically induced imprinting at birth so that they bond intensely with their mothers, the vivid memories and emotions associated with having sex are not easily forgotten[3]. This is by God's design, but it can be a source of torment if we disregard His boundaries for sex. Teenagers intend to move on quickly once their girlfriend or boyfriend breaks up with them, but if they had sex with that person, the lingering mental images will remain as an ongoing reminder of the intimacy they once shared. When the former lover is embracing a new "honey" at the lunch table, the emotional pain and sense of loss can be overwhelming.

Each time young people survive the hurt and devastation of breaking up with someone they've had sex w3ith, they become more preconditioned for divorce. Allow me to reiterate a point I made in Chapter Five—our country's premarital sex statistics and divorce statistics mirror one another. The bonding power of sex is diminished as young people grow familiar with the pain of breaking up with a lover. They become so accustomed to the grieving process that follows parting ways with someone they have had sex with that, upon marriage, the idea of divorce is not foreign to them.

The bonding power of sex is diminished as young people grow familiar with the pain of breaking up with a lover.

REALIZING THE VALUE OF VIRGINITY BEFORE IT'S TOO LATE

Even though I was a young girl at the time, I still remember my mother reaching into her dresser drawer and pulling out a small shiny silver box. I knew the contents had to be valuable because she kept it hidden in an unsuspected place away from the rest of her jewelry. Upon removing the lid, my mother showed me her high school class ring. It was beautiful, but more importantly, the ring was highly sentimental to her.

Sometime later, when I was a freshman in high school, I decided I was going to get that ring out of my mom's dresser and wear it to school. I thought it would be "cool." I knew it wasn't right to sneak behind my mother's back and wear her jewelry, but I convinced myself that it didn't matter since I'd have the ring right back in the box after school.

I managed to keep the ring on most of the day, but during my last class period, a girl started admiring the piece of jewelry, and asked to wear it. I knew her fairly well, so I felt comfortable letting her put it on. Unfortunately I was on my way home from school before I remembered loaning the ring to her. I didn't get too panicked, however, because I figured the girl would just bring it to me the next day.

It was frustrating to get to school the following morning and hear my friend say, "What? I thought I gave it back to you!" My mom's class ring was nowhere to be found. Of course my mother didn't get upset because she didn't know the ring was gone. I felt bad about losing it but thought, "Oh well. It was an old ring anyway—my mother has more valuable jewelry than that."

Three years later, as a senior in high school, it was time to get class rings. My schoolmates and I were beaming with pride as we displayed our "trophies." It was as if all we had accomplished in high school was symbolized in those rings. And then it hit me...*I lost my mother's class ring!* Until I had one of my own, I had no idea how precious a possession that ring truly was. It was a sinking feeling. There was no way to get my mother's ring back. The guilt was overwhelming.

Our virginity is valuable because our future mates are valuable.

And so it is with virginity. When we're young and fancy free, we don't necessarily grasp the value of having never entered into physical intimacy. Eventually we give our virginity away to someone we trust relatively well, and we do so with scarcely enough thought. Just like my mother's class ring, we realize the next day that we can't get our virginity back, but even then, we may not be overly concerned. It's not until we meet the love of our life, that person who is to be our partner for all time, that we realize the magnitude of what we have lost. It is at that point that we also understand how, in giving ourselves to another lover, we let someone else have what belonged exclusively to our mate.

I like to communicate the value of virginity to teenagers by saying, "Your virginity can only be given to *one* person *one* time. That makes it a very special gift! What a joy it is to give that gift to your soul mate as a celebration of your marriage commitment. On the other hand, what a disappointment to have to tell your spouse that you already gave it away."

Simply put, our virginity is valuable because our future mates are valuable.

IN SUMMARY

Let's lovingly remind our children that their virginity is something they can give away in a moment but cannot take back for a lifetime. Let's carefully caution our kids that, after having sex, the image of their nakedness will remain on the minds of the ones who beheld their unclothed bodies long after they put their clothes back on. Let's inspire our teenagers by communicating that they have a once-in-a-lifetime opportunity to save lovemaking, the most physically bonding activity two people can share, for the *one* and *only* person who deserves a gift of that magnitude—their future covenant partner!

In the following chapter, we will look at how to empower young people to determine where to draw the line with "foreplay."

Questions for Thought:

(Before discussing the materials with your child)

1. Can you think of a time when you did things your way instead of God's way and paid a costly price for it? How might hearing that story benefit your child?

2. What are some practical ways that you can remind your child on a regular basis that God has a special mate for him or her and that that person is worth waiting for?

3. What is the most vital concept in the chapter that you want your child to grasp? How do you plan to stress this point?

(After discussing the material with your child):

4. What went really well? What challenges did you have?

5. What have you found to be the most rewarding about discussing the **Parent-Child Discussion Starter** questions?

Parent–Child Discussion Starters

1. When it comes to sex, the Bible tells us (check all that you agree with):
   - ❏ Sex is an evil, dirty act.
   - ❏ Sex is a godly, good act.
   - ❏ Sex is forbidden!
   - ❏ Sex between two married people is blessed.

2. Put an "L" next to the things below that you would look forward to and an "N" next to the things that you would not look forward to:
   - ❏ A dentist appointment
   - ❏ A trip to Disney World
   - ❏ Midterm exams
   - ❏ Meeting your future spouse

3. What do you imagine your future mate might be like? What are some qualities that are important to you?

4. Would you do something if you knew for a fact God did not want you to do it? Why or why not?

5. Do you think Jesus knows what it's like to be tempted sexually? Why or why not?

6. Other than creating children, can you think of a purpose for sex?

7. Have you ever lost something valuable? How did it make you feel?

8. What would it mean to you if your future spouse told you that he/she resisted having sex so that he/she could give his/her virginity to you on your wedding night?

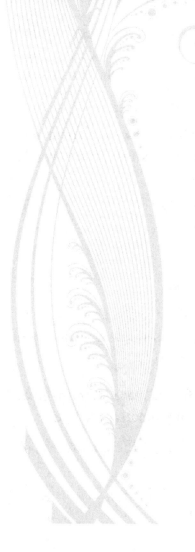

On the other hand, what if he/she said that he/she didn't think you were worth the wait?

9. Where do you think two young people who want to wait until marriage to have sex should draw the line with physical activity?

Discussion Roadmap

1. **When it comes to sex, the Bible tells us (check all that you agree with):**

   ❑ Sex is an evil, dirty act.

   ❑ Sex is a godly, good act.

   ❑ Sex is forbidden!

   ❑ Sex between to married people is blessed.

   Response to all four comments above: sex as God created it is good; it only becomes wicked when God's intended purpose for sex is disregarded (sex outside the boundaries of marriage) (see page 141).

2. **Put an "L" next to the things below that you would look forward to and an "N" next to the things that you would not look forward to:**

   ❑ A dentist appointment

   ❑ A trip to Disney World

   ❑ Mid-term exams

   ❑ Meeting your future spouse

   Explain that inspired abstinence means that we do more than endure being virgins; we anticipate a meaningful reward for our patience (see page 143).

3. **What do you imagine your future mate might be like? What are some qualities that are important to you?**

   a. Listen and discuss each one of the qualities your child listed.

   b. Are there essentials they overlooked, such as spirituality or family values?

   c. Explain that virginity is about saving our hearts and bodies for the *one* person God has for us—our future mates (see page 135). This is exciting!

   d. Read and discuss the Coke Can Principle (story of Tim and his friends) (see pages 136-137).

4. **Would you do something if you knew for a fact that God did not want you to do it? Why or why not?**

   a. Listen and respond to your child's answer.

   b. This is a great time to share a testimony of when you disobeyed God and it cost you.

   c. Explain that God has a mate for each of us, but we can forego God's plan and do things our own way if we want. Discuss the dangers of this (see page 138).

5. **Do you think Jesus knows what it's like to be tempted sexually? Why or why not?**

   a. Explain Hebrews 4:15.

   b. God is aware of our sexuality and all that accompanies our sexual appetites (see page 139).

   c. God's plan for sex is more romantic than society's typical practices (see page 139).

6. **Other than creating children, can you think of a purpose for sex?**

   a. The purpose of sex is to produce a unique bond between two covenant partners (see page 140).

   b. Sex causes chemical reactions that lead to intensified bonding and lingering mental images (see page 141).

   c. Breaking off intimate relationships in one's youth can mentally predispose a person to a divorce when married later in life (see page 141).

7. **Have you ever lost something valuable? How did it make you feel?**

    a. Use "class ring" illustration (see page 142) or other applicable story.

    b. Explain that virginity is often most treasured when we are older and getting married, which is often too late for many young people (see page 143).

8. **What would it mean to you if your future spouse told you that he/she resisted having sex so that he/she could give his/her virginity to you on your wedding night? On the other hand, what if he/she said that he/she didn't think you were worth the wait?**

    a. Explain that our virginity is valuable because our future mates are valuable (see page 143).

    b. Do we want to have to tell our mate we blew it or bless them with the news that we waited?

    c. In light of all they've learned, do they think it's embarrassing to be virgins? Why or why not? How might they deal with peers who scoff at their decision to be abstinent?

9. **Where do you think two young people who want to wait until marriage to have sex should draw the line with physical activity?**

No need to respond to their answers now; this is the topic of the next discussion.

In Summary

☆ Discuss the statements and statistics that are highlighted in boxes throughout the chapter.

☆ Ask your child, "Do you have any questions about what we've discussed today?"

10

FOREPLAY

How Far Is Too Far?

Corresponds with Chapter Five in "Why Wait?"

Yesterday we were discussing sex and dating at the high school girls' Bible study I facilitate each week, and I was surprised to find that many of the young ladies had never heard the term "foreplay." I was also informed that the familiar phrase "making out" is steadily becoming old fashioned and is no longer trendy to use conversationally. The girls clarified that kissing, touching, rubbing, and doing everything but intercourse is now officially referred to as "fooling around." They all giggled when I told them the story of how my best friend in high school was appalled at the term her mom always used—heavy petting.

No matter what we call it, it's important to have discussions with our kids regarding the varying degrees of physical activity in which unmarried couples commonly engage. Kids who have abstinence forced on them will approach the topic with the attitude, "How much can I get away with?" Whereas kids who respect the sacredness of sex and have chosen abstinence for themselves will want to know, "Where should I draw the line in order to maintain sexual purity?"

Seventy-seven percent of teens believe intercourse is the only thing that constitutes as sex and other sexual activities do not count.[1]

The Bible doesn't explicitly define the point when physical activity before marriage becomes sinful, but that's OK—that's not the approach we want to take anyway. We don't want to cater to the "how much can I get away with" crowd. Instead, our goal is to inspire kids with incentives and logical reasons to embrace certain physical boundaries. *The key is to ask questions that lead kids to their own conclusions about where to draw the line as opposed to merely dictating our standards to them.*

WHO'S IN CHARGE HERE?

Perhaps you find it odd that I am encouraging parents to allow their kids to set their own standards regarding physical boundaries. Let me clarify that, as parents, we have an obligation to communicate our expectations to our kids and follow through with consequences should they disregard our stated standards. After all, *parenting is a leadership position*, and all good leaders exercise authority by establishing and enforcing necessary and reasonable expectations for those under their supervision.

Having said this, we *do* need to tell our kids where we expect them to draw the line with physical activity, and failure to meet our expectations should result in consequences. However, *we can't stop here*—our ultimate goal is for our kids to come to their *own* conclusions about where to draw the line, since it is ultimately their convictions, not ours, that motivate their decisions.

"Those" Words

If we're going to communicate clearly with our kids, we have to call things what they are. If you're like me, you may find it terribly uncomfortable to use words like *penis, vagina,* and *sexual climax* in discussions with your teenager—I'm blushing just typing them, much less saying them! If we're not careful, we'll find ourselves resorting to alternative words, such as, a man's "you-know-what," or a woman's "thing-a-ma-jig." In treating sexual terms like curse words that must be substituted with other terms (we say darn in our house instead of damn), we convey an underlying message to our kids that sex is dirty. There's nothing wrong with words like *breasts, ejaculation,* or *libido* unless we are using them in a derogatory or demeaning way. In humankind's perversion, words describing human sexuality are often misused, but that doesn't mean we can't use them correctly—with respect and discretion.

In treating sexual terms like curse words that must be substituted with other terms, we convey an underlying message to our kids that sex is dirty.

Young people appreciate frankness, so make a point to use the actual words and terms that apply to what you are saying. If you're terribly uncomfortable doing this, try saying your least favorite words out loud over and over again until you feel more relaxed about it. (Just make sure no one hears you—that could be awkward!)

It Comes Down to Purpose

In the spirit of inspiring boundaries in our kids instead of merely forcing our convictions on them, let's look at how to lead our kids to their own solid conclusions about where it's best to draw the line with physical affection. From this point on, I'm going to use the term *foreplay* to refer to the various physical activities couples experiment with other than intercourse. You will want to use the word that your teen understands when you discuss this topic with him or her. Once this issue is settled, ask your teen this question,

Is oral sex the same as intercourse in God's eyes? For answers to this question and more, log on to www.InspiringAbstinence.com.

"What is the purpose of foreplay?"

Then be silent and listen. He or she will probably squirm, perhaps even laugh, and say, "I don't know."

Empathize with this uncertainty, but wait for a more solid answer. You can rephrase the question by saying,

"Why do you think your peers engage in foreplay?"

You'll probably hear a response that sounds something like, "They think it feels good," "They want to be close to each other," or, "They are really attracted to each other."

Once your child gives you an answer, acknowledge the validity of the response, and then ask, "What physical reactions take place in the body during foreplay?"

You must now explain to your child that our bodies *physically react* to activities such as kissing, being touched, and feeling someone else's body. Our heart rate picks up, our breathing gets slow and heavy, and blood rushes to our reproductive parts. In a male, sperm cells begin mixing with other bodily secretions making his seed conducive to swimming. During arousal, a woman secretes lubricating vaginal fluids in preparation for intercourse.

Foreplay prepares men and women physically, mentally, and emotionally to have intercourse.

What is the body doing during foreplay? *Preparing for sexual gratification.* Parents, we must stress this point—foreplay prepares men and women physically, mentally, and emotionally to have intercourse. Young people may cite a variety of reasons why they personally participate in foreplay, but our bodies testify to an undeniable purpose of arousal—it gets two people ready to have sex!

With this in mind, we need to ask our kids, "Does it make sense to engage in foreplay, to get physically aroused, if you have no intention of having sexual intercourse?" The obvious conclusion is no.

I've heard school counselors actually encourage kids to explore intimate physical activities and just draw the line at intercourse. They advocate experimenting with arousal. That's a recipe for disaster! All that does is throw logs on the raging fire of a young person's sexual appetite and make sexual intercourse nearly impossible to resist.

It's important to explain to our kids that getting aroused and then slamming on the brakes, which is to cease from physical activity when the body is prepared for sexual intercourse, causes physical discomfort and, in some cases, actual pain and illness. In their book, *Intended For Pleasure,* Ed and Gayle Wheat describe the physical consequences men can expect in such cases:

> If there are repeated episodes of failure to ejaculate, especially following prolonged arousal periods, there can be some injury to the prostate gland, leading to a condition known as prostatitis. This also occurs in men not yet married but engaged in prolonged petting. Symptoms include low-back pain, pelvic pressure, urethral discharge, and slight pain while urinating. The urine is usually free of infection, but the prostate is enlarged, sometimes tense and very tender. [2]

It's not just men who experience a physical backlash from ungratified sexual arousal. During foreplay, a woman experiences an increase in blood supply to her genitals, so much so that they swell to two to three times their normal size. During intercourse, this increased blood supply helps to maximize the sensation of sexual climax, but when climax is never reached, a woman is left feeling uncomfortably bloated. She may also experience throbbing pain in her vaginal area for a couple hours while waiting for the blood supply to subside.

EMOTIONAL DISADVANTAGES OF FOOLING AROUND

Another major consequence of unquenched arousal is the *emotional* toll it takes on young people. If after spending time with a member of the opposite sex, your child is snippy with you, easily angered, and seemingly flustered and frustrated, it may be because he or she has been involved in foreplay. Are you familiar with the term, *sexually frustrated?* When people stir up their sexual appetites without satisfying their physical cravings (i.e. no intercourse), they often become hostile, aggravated, and frustrated because of the emotional letdown and hormonal deluge they experience. Simply put, it's not natural for the body to get ready to have sex and then not have it.

More than half of teens ages 15-19 say they've had oral sex.[3]

Are there other ways to achieve climax without having intercourse? Yes, but now we're blatantly looking for creative ways to get around God's boundaries for sex. Remember, we have no business enjoying the benefits of sexual gratification without the covenant commitment (review Chapter Five if need be). To drive home this point, I often ask young people, "Do you want your future spouse pursing alternatives to intercourse that still allow him or her to experience sexual climax with a girlfriend or boyfriend?" Of course they don't. As a general rule, if physical contact is causing sexual climax, two unmarried people have gone too far.

Seventy-eight percent of new cases of genital herpes were caused by a virus found chiefly in the mouths of 16-21 year olds [i.e., acquired though oral sex].[4]

Just like the sight of a steak makes a hungry man salivate, foreplay makes a person desperate for intercourse. Even kissing can cause tremendous sexual arousal. Knowing that sex is sacred and that fooling around prepares the body, mind, and emotions to have sex, ask your son or daughter, "What is the purpose of fooling around if you don't plan on having sex?" Help your child to see that there is no purpose. Furthermore, foreplay will only do one of two things:

1. Set us up for aggravation and disappointment because our intense desires go unmet.

2. Set us up to go all the way.

A VALUABLE LESSON FROM MOSQUITO BITES

What's the first thing most moms say when their children come indoors complaining about an itchy mosquito bite? "Don't scratch it!" Kind of ironic, isn't it? The only thing that brings some relief from the nagging pain is to scratch the bite, and that's the one thing moms asks kids not to do. What children often don't realize about the pesky itch of a mosquito bite, however, is that *scratching it only makes it itch more.* The momentary liberation we feel while we scratch is followed by a greater sensation of itchiness.

Believe it or not, we can learn an extremely valuable lesson from mosquito bites. When a young person feels a strong sense of attraction toward a member of the opposite sex, he starts "itching" to have physical contact with her. Initially, just holding hands with her is enough to soothe his desires. Pretty soon though, clutching her hand becomes commonplace, and the itching returns. He can't stop staring at her glossed lips and envisioning them pressed against his. And oh how his stomach flip-flops the day that she kisses him in the school parking lot! Some days later, however, those quick after school kisses don't bring quite the excitement they used to, and once again he is itching for more, only now his physical longings have intensified. He wants a "real" kiss—a long passionate French kiss. He wonders if the world has stopped spinning the first time he gets one. Wow! What an experience! Unfortunately, three weeks later, those long kisses don't quite "cure the itch" for him anymore. He now wants so badly to feel her body pressed against his.

Whereas intercourse leads to a gloriously fulfilling conclusion, foreplay leads couples to an ever-increasing feeling of discontent and longing to go further.

Do you see where I'm going with this? Young people think that if they can just go to the next physical level, just "scratch the itch," they will be satisfied, but they soon find out that it only leaves them wanting more. Whereas sexual intercourse leads to a gloriously fulfilling conclusion, foreplay leads couples to an ever-increasing feeling of discontent and longing to go further.

When young people are contemplating where to draw the line, they must understand that the more liberty they give themselves, the more difficult they are actually making things. As a general rule, *the further we go, the further we want to go.* Obviously as a couple increases their level of physical interaction, it gets more difficult to resist going all the way. And what happens if a young lady is ready to stop but her boyfriend isn't?

A dear friend of mine fought back the tears while sharing her testimony with a small group of high school girls. She explained that as a teenage girl, she and an attractive young man were fooling around one evening at his house while his parents were gone. She enjoyed the kissing and touching, but eventually felt that things were going too far. She told him she wanted to stop, but he refused to listen to her. With a horrifying forcefulness he proceeded to have sexual intercourse with her, totally ignoring her objections. She lost her virginity, not because she was ready to give it away, but because an aroused young man was not willing to let his desires go unmet.

Reciting this woman's testimony, I often warn young ladies, "It's not just about how far *you* can go and still resist going all the way; your partner may insist you've gone too far to stop!" When a man takes advantage of a woman under these circumstances, it's referred to as date rape. Even though it is unlawful, unfortunately it's nearly impossible to enforce legal consequences—if a guy insists it was mutual sex, how can a young lady prove otherwise?

PRINCIPLES OF BOUNDARY SETTING

Young people need to decide where they want to draw the line with physical activity *before* they find themselves in a passionate make-out session. The more specific the boundaries are, the less chance there is for gray areas that lead to compromise. Once identified, these standards must be clearly communicated with whomever a young person is dating. Obviously, if our kids' boundaries are mocked, met with contempt, or openly rejected by a member of the opposite sex, they have no business dating that person. Both parties should be equally committed to abiding by physical boundaries.

Some examples of boundaries two young people might commit to are:

☆ Kisses are "pecks" on the cheeks, not open mouth kisses on the lips.

☆ We never lay down together—we're upright at all times.

☆ Our hands do not touch private parts or "wander" around.

☆ We're never at each other's houses when parents aren't home.

☆ We don't hang out alone in the car; once we arrive at our destination, we get out.

TO KISS OR NOT TO KISS

Before I go on to the next step in the boundary setting process, allow me to address the issue of kissing. Kissing is something young people tend to think nothing about, which is to say, they consider it a perfectly acceptable, if not an expected part of a dating relationship. However, a kiss can be very passionate and can easily ignite sexual arousal. Traditionally, kissing is viewed as "no big deal," but in reality, it can be quite an intimate and bonding experience. Knowing this, it's important that our kids do not simply follow the masses in this area. Sure, society will make fun of anyone that says they want to wait until they are married to French kiss, but then again, society is being devastated by divorce, infidelity, STDs, and unwanted pregnancies—hardly the crowd we want to take advice from.

Our kids don't have to engage in passionate kissing just because it's socially acceptable.

My point is that, even though it can sound a bit extreme in our culture to say that we don't want to kiss until we're married, it truly is a wise decision. It's not a choice that can be forced on young people, but should they make this decision for themselves, it is to be admired. As parents, we should let our kids know that they don't have to engage in passionate kissing just because it's socially acceptable. They have a choice, a wonderful opportunity to set their own standards based on their ideas about love and future romance.

ACCOUNTABILITY: THE KEY TO KEEPING BOUNDARIES

Identifying physical boundaries is one thing; keeping them is another. Ironically, determining off-limit intimacy levels can actually cause temptation to escalate! Experience tells us that "forbidden fruit" tends to provoke humanity's lust.

When faced with a wave of sexual longing, young couples often get swept off their feet, unexpectedly forsaking their boundary commitments. Due to inexperience, they underestimate temptation's powerful pull. How quickly it can engulf one's good intentions and promises! Furthermore, a drowning man is in no position to rescue the lady drowning next to him. *This is why third-party accountability is so important.*

Once a couple has clearly defined sexual boundaries, they should share their commitment with an outside source—a "lifeguard" of sorts who will keep an eye on their relationship and blow the whistle if things get out of hand. This person is not being nosey. On the contrary, he or she is empowered by the couple to stay aware, informed, and connected to the relationship as a continual source of encouragement and accountability.

Should two young people find themselves tempted to compromise, they know they can go to their accountability partner for counsel and prayer. They also know it won't be long before their accountability partner approaches them and asks some forthright questions, such as, "How well are you two maintaining your physical boundaries?" "Have you been struggling lately?" "How much time are you two spending alone with each other?"

When a young person knows he will give account for his actions to someone he admires and respects, it can throw a wet blanket on the fiery embers of temptation.

When a young person knows he will give account for his actions to someone he admires and respects, it can throw a wet blanket on the fiery embers of temptation. Since he dreads the thought of admitting he went back on his commitment, he becomes apprehensive in those crucial moments when he feels the urge to push past physical boundaries. Having an accountability partner can make all the difference in the moment of decision.

Every couple who chooses abstinence needs ongoing accountability, someone who will not only keep up with how the relationship is progressing emotionally, but will continually ask how things are going *physically*, in terms of maintaining their stated boundaries. For teenagers, this should not be a peer relationship, but rather a mature adult who will motivate them in their commitment.

In a perfect world, kids would always look to their parents to fill this role, but it is often the case that they must look elsewhere for support. I have gladly stepped in and served in this capacity for teenagers. Here are some tips for serving as an accountability partner to your child or another young person:

- ☆ If possible, get together with both the young man and young woman who are in the relationship. If only one of them is willing to subject themselves to this kind of accountability, lovingly point out that the relationship is already at risk. They both need to be in agreement about the boundary process if it's going to be effective.

- ☆ Ask that they write down their physical boundaries and submit a copy to you. Discuss what practical steps they are going to take to ensure they uphold them.

- ☆ Explain that you will ask them about their relationship on a regular basis as a means of accountability. Also let them know that they can come to you anytime they want to talk.

- ☆ Let them know in advance that if their relationship becomes increasingly physical and there is legitimate concern that they may have sex, you will have to contact their parents. Otherwise you will maintain strict confidentiality.

- ☆ Get to know the couple and build a relationship with them. Perhaps have them over for dinner occasionally, or go out and enjoy a recreational activity with them now and again. The better you get to know them, the more comfortable you will all feel about your role.

- ☆ If your spouse is available to be involved too, that's an added benefit.

- ☆ Young people can be extremely irresponsible and do not always stay in contact like they intend to, but you will want to diligently stay in touch with the couple. In addition to asking how they are doing in a general sense, you want to regularly ask straightforward questions about the physical aspect of their relationship. Encourage them and pray with them often.

☆ If you find that they are pushing past their physical boundaries, bring them together for a meeting and reestablish the purpose behind their commitment. Help to reignite their passion for abstinence. If they continue to push past their boundaries, let them know that you have no choice but to talk with their parents.

☆ Obviously kids can lie to you and cover up their behavior, but that is their choice and beyond your control. You are there to help them carry out their commitment to abstinence, but it is ultimately their commitment to keep.

If you are serving as your child's accountability partner, a great exercise is to have him decide in advance what consequences are fair and logical if boundaries are crossed. Put these consequences in writing. Then, if your child confesses to having compromised his stated standards, you can enforce the consequences you two previously agreed upon.

Since premarital sex and dating tend to go hand-in-hand, our next chapter will answer the question, "What should I teach my child about dating?"

Questions for Thought:

(Before discussing the material with your child):

1. Explain why it's important that our kids be empowered to decide where to draw the line with physical activity. What stipulations do you plan to enforce?

2. Would you feel comfortable being an accountability partner for your child's dating relationship? Why or why not?

3. What is the most vital concept in the chapter that you want your child to grasp? How do you plan to stress this point?

(After discussing the material with your child):

4. What challenges did you have during the discussion? What went well?

5. Are there any points from the previous chapters that you sense your child didn't grasp? How might you go back and better explain those concepts?

Parent–Child Discussion Starters

1. In your opinion, what is the purpose of foreplay?

2. What do you think physically occurs in a male's body when he becomes aroused? What happens in a female's body?

3. How do you think it affects a young person's mood and emotions when he or she comes close to having sex but "slams on the brakes" (i.e. no sexual intercourse)?

4. In your opinion, does fooling around satisfy a couple's sexual longings? Why or why not?

5. Where do you specifically think it's wise to draw the line with physical activity?

6. TRUE or FALSE: It is not possible to get sexually aroused from French kissing. _____

7. Once a couple decides they don't want to have premarital sex, what are some practical ways they can guard against going too far?

Discussion Roadmap

1. **In your opinion, what is the purpose of foreplay?**

   a. Explain that our bodies physically respond to foreplay (see page 153).

   b. Stress that foreplay prepares the body for intercourse (see page 154).

2. **What do you think physically occurs in a male's body when he becomes aroused? What happens in a female's body?**

   a. Site specific physical reactions for each gender (see page 155).

   b. Explain that our bodies were not created to get aroused and then "slam on the brakes" (see page 155)

   c. Read Ed and Gayle Wheat's description of what unquenched arousal can lead to (see page 155).

3. **How do you think it affects young people's moods and emotions when they come close to having sex but "slam on the brakes" (i.e. no intercourse)?**

   a. When people stir up their sexual appetite without satisfying their physical cravings (i.e. no intercourse), they often become hostile, aggravated, and frustrated, because of the emotional letdown and hormonal deluge they experience (see page 156).

   b. It's not natural for the body to get ready to have sex and then not have it (see page 157).

   c. Just like the sight of a steak makes a hungry man salivate, foreplay makes a person desperate for intercourse.

   d. Pursing alternative methods for achieving climax means we are blatantly looking for ways to get around God's boundaries for sex (see page 158).

4. **In your opinion, does fooling around satisfy a couple's sexual longings? Why or why not?**

   a. Discuss your child's answer.

   b. Use "mosquito bite" illustration—the further we go, the further we want to go (see page 158).

   c. Explain that foreplay only intensifies our longings, versus satisfying them (see page 158).

5. **Where do you specifically think it's wise to draw the line with physical activity?**

   a. Share "date rape" testimony out of book—explain that it is unwise for young ladies to arouse a guy when she has no intention of going all the way (see page 158).

   b. Explain that boundaries need to be established *before* temptation comes (see page 158).

   c. Explain that boundaries should be written down and agreed upon by anyone your child chooses to date (see page 159).

   d. Make a written list of practical physical boundaries your child wants to keep.

6. **TRUE or FALSE: It is not possible to get sexually aroused from French kissing.**

   a. Kissing among unmarried young people is a common practice, but it doesn't have to be (see page 159).

   b. Kissing can be extremely arousing (see page 160).

   c. Encourage your child to decide if it is worth it to engage in kissing before marriage and to not let society decide for him/her.

7. **Once a couple decides they don't want to have premarital sex, what are some practical ways they can guard against going too far?**

a. Discuss the concept and benefits of having third-party accountability (see page 160).

b. Discuss practical boundaries, such as going out in groups and only spending time with members of the opposite sex in public places (this question is geared to get your child thinking about issues that will be discussed in the following chapter).

c. Is your child willing to treat members of the opposite sex as his/her brothers/sisters in Christ?

In Summary

☆ Perhaps discuss the statements and statistics that are highlighted in boxes throughout the chapter.

☆ Ask your child, "Do you have any questions about what we've discussed today?"

DATING

What About Dating?

Corresponds with Chapter Six in "Why Wait?"

What do money, handguns, and dating relationships have in common? They can be a blessing or a curse, depending upon how we handle them. Mom or Dad, when it comes to dating, our kids need more from us than cash and curfews—they need guidance, practical wisdom, and clearly defined boundaries. Just as the quality of a building's foundation determines its long-term stability, the way our children approach dating can have a lasting impact on their future relationships. For this reason, we must take the time to provide our kids with insight and knowledge about dating.

THE DEFINITION OF DATING

Dating is one of those concepts that means different things to different people. It's important, when talking to our kids, that we first identify what they consider to be a dating relationship. From there, we can explain that dating, in its simplest form, refers to a man and a woman getting to know each other. *The pivotal factor here is the **degree** that we choose to get to know a member of the opposite sex.*

Each failed intimate relationship makes a significant withdraw from our soul, which can bankrupt us long before we ever enter into marriage.

Intimacy occurs when we give someone access to the most personal, vulnerable aspects of who we are. In intimate relationships, we give *ourselves* to others. Furthermore, the more intimate our premarital relationships are, the more of ourselves we give away.

Teenage "dating" websites that boast millions of members encourage teenage patrons to select not prom dates but partners for casual sexual escapades.[1]

The danger of our culture's current dating trend is that it encourages young people to hold nothing back, to totally give themselves physically and emotionally to whomever they are dating at the time—as if, by some miracle boomerang effect, their acts of vulnerability will be returned to them when the relationship ends. In reality, each failed intimate relationship makes a significant withdrawal from our soul, which can bankrupt us long before we ever enter into marriage. As our soul "account" dwindles, so does our ability to freely trust, love, forgive, and commit to someone for life.

Now let's not overlook the fact that it can be advantageous for young people in their later teens to get socially acquainted with the opposite sex. When guys and gals cultivate friendships with each other, it helps them understand and relate to how "the other half" lives. It also gives them a glimpse of the qualities they do and do not want in a mate someday. However, this does not mean that young people should pursue *serious commitments* with one member of the opposite sex after another, which has few benefits, if any, and a myriad of possible negative consequences.

As with all of life's issues, *the key to dating is balance.* Since our culture's dating practices are so very out of balance, it is imperative that we take an objective look at the subject. By objective, I mean we must be willing to compare worldly dating trends with God's wisdom and standards.

We do not want our kids to totally isolate themselves from the opposite sex, nor do we want them entangled in overly intimate relationships. Here are some practical ways to keep relationships with the opposite sex balanced:

Don't start dating too early.

Do not stir up nor awaken love until it pleases (Song of Solomon 2:7).

Throughout the Book of Song of Solomon, we are repeatedly warned not to stir up or awaken love until it pleases, meaning that it is not wise to prematurely incite a young person's desire for romance or sexual appetite. Nothing, and I stress, *not one good thing,* comes from letting 13, 14, or 15-year-old kids go out on dates. Sixteen may very well be too young also, depending on the individual maturity level of your teenager. If young teens want to attend a supervised social function with a group of friends, that's one thing. But two smitten junior high kids have no business going to the movies alone (or anywhere else for that matter)! Even freshmen and sophomores in high school usually lack the maturity to handle the pressures and emotions that accompany dating.

Twenty-five percent of girls and 30 percent of boys have sex by age 15; 21 percent of 9th graders have slept with four or more partners.[2]

There is no formulaic way to determine exactly when your teenager is adequately prepared to handle spending time with the opposite sex. The best we can do is to ask ourselves, "Is my teenager responsible, decisive, trustworthy, obedient, spiritually astute, and confident in his or her convictions?" If the answer is yes, we can proceed with caution and rely on the Holy Spirit to guide us as we make daily decisions regarding our teens' dating desires and requests. If the answer is no, let's get busy cultivating these character qualities in our kids through discipleship.

Once our teenagers blossom into young adults and become steadily more independent from us, the decision to date becomes theirs and not ours. Knowing this, we can't afford to be complacent parents during our kids' formidable years lest they enter adulthood lacking the spiritual maturity and strength of character to cultivate healthy relationships with the opposite sex.

Early sexual experiences correlate with depression and drug use.[3]

If our adolescent and mid-teen kids nag about why they aren't allowed to date yet, we can remind them that God has a mate in mind for them to spend the rest of their lives with—surely it is a waste of time and energy to start looking for this person a decade or so before they are even ready for marriage!

"Who said anything about finding a mate? I just want to have a good time!" If that's your child's attitude, encourage her to go rent a movie with buddies or go to the mall with her best friend, but don't let her start dating too early just because she's bored! Cultivating healthy dating relationships requires that we have the maturity to set and maintain some very important boundaries—why not give ourselves some time before we take on this responsibility?

Keep dating relationships casual.

Just as an inheritance gained in haste does not prosper its recipient in the long-run, relationships formed through premature intimacy and rushed commitments are not equipped to stand the test of time. Unfortunately, there is an increasing trend among young people—they tend to think of relationships with the opposite sex as an "all or nothing" proposition. As a result, our modern-day teenagers are either mere acquaintances with certain members of the opposite sex or are wrapped up in serious, all-consuming, committed relationships—there's very little middle ground.

An inheritance gained hastily at the beginning will not be blessed at the end (Proverbs 20:21).

There are a variety of reasons I suspect this is occurring. Premature sexual activity, increased jealousies and insecurities, Hollywood's deceptive influence, and our culture's tendency toward impatience are all likely contributing factors. The end result, however, is that kids are missing out on the central benefit of dating—*cultivating quality friendships with members of the opposite sex without the entanglement of serious commitments.*

Let's encourage our kids that they can spend time with an attractive member of the opposite sex in social settings, enjoy having lunch together at school, and talk on the phone now and then, but it is not beneficial in the long run to spend every waking moment consumed with the relationship! Young people need to know that it is possible to get to know someone without making a serious commitment. They don't have to pursue deep levels of emotional and physical connection simply because that's the expectation and norm these days.

Let's inform our kids that, just because they are attracted to someone, it does not mean that they have to take the relationship to the next level. As a matter of fact, they can appreciate the way someone looks without taking any action at all.

I often ask young people, "What is the purpose of committing to be an exclusive couple, avoiding all other members of the opposite sex, when you are too young to pursue marriage?" If the truth be told, these kinds of "forsake all other" commitments most often result when teen couples become so involved that they can't tolerate the idea of seeing their "honey" interested in anyone else. So, they commit solely to each other, which usually creates a variety of problems (also known as "drama"). He anxiously wonders, *Why was she walking with Johnny after third period yesterday? She worries, Is it true that Sally told Jenny that Amy saw Jessica and my boyfriend exchange phone numbers on the bus this morning?*

Teenage committed relationships are often an exhausting roller-coaster of emotional ups and downs because the relationship is in a "limbo" of sorts. The two teens are like a married couple in some ways, but not in others. They have the same monogamous standard and protective jealousy as married couples, yet they lack the assurance and security that married people enjoy—a lifelong commitment signified through marriage vows. In most teen relationships, all it takes is a tough day, a misunderstood note, or an attractive new student in science class, and suddenly the relationship is in jeopardy!

Such relationships can suck all the fun out of a young person's single years, the time when he or she should be meeting all kinds of interesting people and having a blast with friends, who, by the way, often fall to the wayside when a boyfriend or girlfriend enters the scene.

I'm not advocating a philosophy that says, "Son, commit to no one; just play the field and go from one girl to the next." I'm talking about staying on the sidelines all together. Our kids shouldn't isolate themselves from the opposite sex, but they don't need to fill up their lives with them either. Keep it simple! Keep it casual!

> Even if a baby of a teen mother is born healthy, he or she is still likely to experience numerous complications later on, including poor health; inadequate education; low intelligence; and anger at his or her family, community, and society.[4]

Don't isolate.

As previously mentioned, young people often neglect their family relationships and friendships once a boyfriend or girlfriend comes along. They spend every waking moment with their "sweetie," isolating themselves from other key relationships in their lives. As parents, we have every right to draw the line if we feel our child's priorities are spiraling out of control (providing that they are under 18 years of age). I've seen situations where a young person's spiritual commitments, grades, friendships, and extra-curricular activities take a drastic plunge because he is so focused on a love interest. In situations like these, we can limit how much time our kids spend out of the house, on the computer, or talking on the phone with their boyfriend or girlfriend. It's essential, however, that we go about it the right way.

A man who isolates himself seeks his own desire; he rages against all wise judgment (Proverbs 18:1).

Explain to your child that it is your responsibility as a parent to set boundaries that keep her balanced and on track with her priorities. In the spirit of inspiring our kids, versus merely enforcing policies, we should strive to help our kids understand the valid motivations and purposes for our boundary setting. Here's an example of how to do this. Suppose you become concerned that your son is too focused on a particular girl (or that your daughter is overly consumed with a certain young man). Have him write down his priorities in order, starting with what is his highest priority. Then lovingly help him see how his stated priorities are suffering as a result of overly focusing on his girlfriend, and that, by making a few changes, some major improvements can occur. If he recognizes the benefits and reasoning of your boundaries, he is likely to appreciate them and therefore embrace them without a great deal of reluctance. If not, you still have a right to stick to your boundaries. It is often the case that we hear "thanks Mom and Dad!" later in life, when our kids are no longer kids.

Throughout puberty, bodies add bone, redistribute weight, and gain height, while the inner organs (including the uterus) mature. Pregnancy interferes with this, because another set

of hormones directs the body to sustain new life. Nature protects the fetus, which may take essential nutrients (especially calcium and iron) from the mother. If normal pubescent growth is deflected, that causes the girl to become a shorter and sicker woman than she otherwise would have been.[5]

Discourage your teenager from neglecting his friends as a result of focusing all of his time, energy, and attention on his girlfriend. Chances are, he and his girlfriend will break up someday, and he will wish he had not run off all of his friends. Buddies usually don't come back around too easily after being discarded for a girl.

If your teenager chooses to have a girlfriend, it's beneficial for him to go out in groups and spend time in social settings involving his friends *and* his girlfriend. Having friends around helps keep him out of physically compromising situations and will also give him a better idea of what kind of girl he's dating. If she can't stand his friends, the people he loves to hang around, perhaps the two of them are not going to be compatible in the long run.

Guard your heart.

Have you ever met someone who seemed like his life was out of control? We often say of that kind of person, "He's got issues!" The Bible tells us where our *issues* come from—the heart (mind, will, and emotions), which is why we have to diligently protect it. The emphasis of this book is about inspiring our kids to guard their bodies from premature sexual activity, but the Bible also warns us to guard our *hearts*.

Keep [guard] your heart with all diligence, for out of it spring the issues of life (Proverbs 4:23).

If I've seen it once, I've seen it a hundred times. A young girl experiences mutual attraction and starts spending more and more time with a handsome young man. At first their conversations are about silly things and are peppered with giggles and sighs. But in time, they both start opening up and sharing more personal testimonies—past hurts, current fears, future dreams, and aspirations. As they trust each other with their most vulnerable memories, thoughts, and feelings, powerful bonds of intimacy are formed.

Eventually a falling out occurs and the couple splits up. Unfortunately they have no way of taking back the emotional investment they made in each other. In such cases, the pain of breaking up is devastating for young people and can negatively affect their grades, friendships, sleep patterns, eating habits, and other significant aspects of their lives.

Another incentive to guard our hearts is that, when we make strong emotional connections with members of the opposite sex, physical temptation intensifies. However, even if two young people manage to protect their relationship from *physical* intimacy, they still run the risk of forming damaging "soul ties" based on an over abundance of *emotional* intimacy. Soul ties are the mental and emotional strings that keep us connected to someone long after we have parted ways.

I have counseled ladies over the years who are married, have a house full of children, but live with nagging feelings of attachment toward certain men from their past. Particular songs, scents, or familiar settings can trigger a flood of memories and emotions. In those moments, a woman desires more than anything to somehow connect with the man she bonded with in her youth.

While soul ties can be a surefire recipe for infidelity, they are also a source of ongoing torment as men and women struggle to overcome the mental and emotional battles when memories of "old flames" ignite. And consider how hurtful it is for a spouse to learn that his or her mate has recurring feelings for someone else! It undermines the foundation of trust on which relationships are built.

Inspired abstinence is just as much about saving our hearts for our future mates as it is about saving our bodies. Young people need to be encouraged to guard their hearts and protect themselves from emotions and experiences that can ultimately cause regret and anguish. To reiterate a point made earlier, when we share our heart with someone, in essence, we are giving ourselves away. Just like we can't un-ring a bell, we can't undo the emotional intimacy we create with someone. This is another reason why dating relationships should be kept casual.

Don't get caught up in missionary dating!

We've all seen it, if not lived it. Some sweet girl with a big heart and naive mind latches on to a down-and-outer. "He needs my help," she tells concerned loved ones. In an effort to rehabilitate him, she stays in the relationship even though it revolves almost entirely around him and his constant needs. She holds onto the hope that her love will somehow change him. Time drags on and everyone *except her* sees the writing on the wall—he's taking advantage of her good intentions and dragging her down with him.

Do not be unequally yoked together with unbelievers (2 Corinthians 6:14).

Dating someone in an effort to somehow modify his or her behavior is often referred to as "missionary dating." I've noticed that Christian kids can be especially susceptible to this. I could give this book away for free if I had a nickel for every time a young girl started her conversation with me by saying, "I'm a Christian, and I'm trying to get my boyfriend to accept Christ." Guys do the same thing. They think God is calling them to date a girl in order to influence her spiritual beliefs and win her to the Lord.

We need to inform our kids that Scripture actually warns against this. Second Corinthians 6:14 tells us not be unequally yoked with unbelievers. Upon hearing this passage, we tend to envision egg yolk and wonder what in the world this Scripture means. Actually, that's not the kind of yoke God is referring to here. He's talking about the harness placed around two animals' necks, like oxen for example, used to keep them side by side while they plow up and down a field. This binding yoke forces two animals to take the same path.

One quality missionary daters tend to have in common is that they truly believe that they are the only hope their boyfriend or girlfriend has.

When God tells us not to be unequally yoked, He's telling us not to join ourselves in a committed relationship with an unbeliever. Our Master has a path for us to travel, and we don't want to hook up with someone who isn't ready or willing to go in the direction where we are called. With this in mind, we have no business entering into romantic relationships in an effort to help or change someone.

One quality missionary daters tend to have in common is that they truly believe that they are the *only* hope their boyfriend or girlfriend has. They are convinced that, if they break it off, their needy companion will spiral out of control. In this way, missionary daters suffer from false guilt, erroneously concluding that the other person's well-being, future, and perhaps eternal destination is dependent on their own ability to love, care, and transform that person. This is a deceptive lie!

A troubled young man doesn't need the mentorship of a girlfriend; he needs a godly man in his life. Along those same lines, a distressed young lady doesn't need a boyfriend to coach her through her issues. She needs a mature spiritual mother to come along and minister to her. God knows this and is well able to orchestrate a plan that involves bringing the right people along at the right time. We don't need to "help God" by attempting to rescue members of the opposite sex though the avenue of dating relationships.

It's easier for someone to push us off of a stool than it is for us to pull someone up onto a stool with us. Likewise, missionary daters are much more likely to be negatively influenced by their troubled counterpart than they are to actually motivate lasting change in their boyfriend or girlfriend.

Each year, one in ten girls under the age of 20—one million per year—becomes pregnant; 40 percent of these pregnancies will end in abortion.[6]

Protect dating relationships from physical activity.

Just as I started to type this section's subtitle, I was interrupted and took a break from writing—the reason is slightly ironic. A distraught young lady called to tell me that she and her boyfriend of six months just broke up. The reason? They have not been respecting each other's physical boundaries, and it's taken a terrible toll on the relationship. Instead of the lighthearted fun this Christian couple used to enjoy together, they are now plagued by stress, guilt, confusion, and resentment toward each other. As a result, he called this morning to tell her that he can't continue the relationship, leaving her full of regret and disappointment.

The break-up prompted this young lady to have an honest and open talk with her parents, during which she confessed everything she's been doing in the relationship. They have now committed to take a more active role providing boundaries and accountability for their daughter in the future, which is great. Still, the lesson is clear—if you want to take a perfectly good relationship and ruin it, just disregard God's sexual standards. For the many reasons stated throughout this book, premarital sexual activity is not wise, even if it's just "fooling around."

POINTERS FOR PARENTS

Here are some pointers that may come in handy as you encounter your teenager's dating years:

Get to know the person your son or daughter is dating.

There is a tight connection between teen girls' sexual behavior and dating older boys.[7]

This will give you a better idea of what kind of boundaries need to be established. For example, if the young man your daughter is dating is immature spiritually and behaviorally, you know that allowing him to drive her to and from their destination might not be such a good idea. Have game nights, go out to dinner, or play a round of miniature golf, just make sure you include your son or daughter and his or her date from time to time. This not only provides them with a temptation-free environment, but it also affords you the right to share any concerns you may have about the relationship. Our kids are much more likely to respect our opinions about the person they are dating if we've actually taken the time to get to know them (at the conclusion of this chapter, we'll look at how to recognize the warning signs of unhealthy dating relationships).

Promote group activities.

When our kids ask us if they can go out on a date, it's wise to grant them permission with the condition that they include a few friends. Group activities are a great way to guard the relationship against premature intimacy and to keep friendships intact (versus abandoning friendships for a dating relationship). Going out in groups can act as an "intimacy guard" of sorts and helps to keep dating relationships casual, versus overly personal and romantic.

State your house rules in advance.

Here are a few suggested guidelines you might want to give your son or daughter:

- ☆ No member of the opposite sex is allowed in your bedroom.
- ☆ Once we go to bed, your date has to go home.
- ☆ The door to the TV room is never closed if you're watching a movie in there with a member of the opposite sex.
- ☆ (If your teenager is permitted to ride alone in a car with his or her date) No hanging out in the car or driveway. Come inside with your date or tell him goodbye.

☆ No member of the opposite sex is allowed in the house if we are not home.

Can you think of any more house rules you personally might want to establish? A great way to inspire our kids to embrace our house rules is to ask them to come up with their own list of rules before revealing ours. We can then compare lists, discuss the rationale behind the boundaries we each came up with, and develop our official house rules together, as a team. This doesn't mean we compromise our boundaries to meet our kids' approval. However, by listening to their opinions, considering their suggestions, and explaining why we believe certain standards are necessary, we are extending respect to our teenagers. This tends to evoke a reciprocation of respect from them in the form of submissive obedience, which is quite nice!

Talk to the parents.

Before your teenager goes over to her boyfriend's house, make sure you talk to the young man's parents. Share your house rules and see if they will agree to respect your same boundaries when your daughter is over there (the same applies to our sons).

We often erroneously assume that all parents, especially those who profess Christianity, maintain our same standards and supervision measures, but this is not so. Just the other day a woman tearfully explained to me that she recently learned that for the last several months, her 14-year-old daughter has been having sex while over at her boyfriend's house. This mother trusted that the boy's parents were watching the couple as closely as she always did at her house. Unfortunately she was wrong. She later learned that the boy's parents assumed the kids were too young to actually go all the way—*wrong!* This brings me to my final point.

Don't be naive.

I cannot tell you how many times I've heard parents say, "I can't believe my child is sexually active! She's such a good girl!" Case in point, we often erroneously believe that, because our kids are good kids, they are not going to make a bad choice to have premarital sex. Perhaps we even have a good feeling about the "sweetheart" they've been running around with, and we think, *Those two would never do something that irresponsible.* That is a naïve parental mindset. If two young people are attracted to each other, they have the propensity to have sex—I don't care how responsible or mature they are for their age. Obviously the principles in this book are designed to inspire our kids to embrace abstinence, but in our parental role, we must supply the proper amount of supervision. We can't give our kids an over-abundance of leeway in dating relationships because we naively believe, *My kid would never give in to temptation.*

RELATIONSHIP SELF-TEST

Below you will see a checklist that serves as an excellent tool for our teens to evaluate the health of their dating relationships. Simply put, if a dating relationship is not healthy, it is not God's will that two people proceed with marriage. (Reminder, **Questions for Thought** are listed after the Relationship Self-Test.)

Is my relationship healthy?

Check the box if you and the person you're seeing…

- ❏ Have fun together most of the time.
- ❏ Each enjoy spending time separately, with your own friends, as well as with each other's friends.
- ❏ Always feel safe with each other.
- ❏ Trust each other.
- ❏ Are faithful to each other (if you have made this commitment).
- ❏ Support each other's individual goals in life, like ministry, education, or career goals.
- ❏ Respect each other's opinions, even when they are different.

❏ Solve conflicts without putting each other down, cursing at each other, or making threats.

❏ Enjoy spiritually beneficial conversations that center around the truth of God's Word.

❏ Both accept responsibility for your actions.

❏ Both apologize when you're wrong.

❏ Both have decision-making power in the relationship.

❏ Are proud to be with each other.

❏ Encourage each other's interests like sports and leisure activities.

❏ Have some privacy—your letters, journals, and personal phone calls are respected as your own.

❏ Have close friends and relatives who are happy about your relationship.

❏ Never feel like you're being pressured for sex.

❏ Always allow each other "space" when you need it.

❏ Always treat each other with respect.

Is my relationship unhealthy?

Check the box if one of you...

❏ Gets extremely jealous or accuses the other of cheating or wanting to cheat.

❏ Puts the other down by calling names, cursing, or making the other feel bad about himself or herself.

❏ Yells or speaks in harsh tones.

❏ Doesn't take the other person, or things that are important to him/her, seriously.

❏ Doesn't listen when the other talks.

❏ Frequently criticizes the other's friends or family.

❏ Pressures the other for sex.

❏ Has ever threatened to hurt the other or commit suicide if the other leaves.

❏ Cheats or threatens to cheat.

❏ Is into pornography.

❏ Tells the other how to dress.

❏ Is opposed to or makes fun of the other's commitment to Christ or involvement with church.

❏ Acts one way at church but another way outside of church.

❏ Has ever grabbed, pushed, hit, or physically hurt the other.

❏ Blames the other for own behavior ("If you wouldn't have made me mad, I wouldn't have …").

❏ Embarrasses or humiliates the other.

❏ Smashes, throws, or destroys things.

❏ Tries to keep the other from having commitments and ambitions, such as a job or education goals.

❏ Makes all the decisions about what the two of you do.

❏ Tries to make the other feel crazy or plays mind games.

❏ Goes back on promises and regularly does not keep his/her word.

❏ Acts controlling or possessive.

❏ Uses alcohol or drugs.

❏ Ignores or withholds affection as a way of punishing the other.

❏ Depends completely on the other to meet social or emotional needs.

Questions for Thought

(Before discussing the material with your child):

1. Do you think your child is ready to date? Why or why not?

2. What issue(s) are you the most concerned about in regard to your child dating?

3. Based on the directives mentioned in the "Pointers for Parents" section, are there certain changes or improvements you need to make?

(After discussing the material with your child):

4. What challenges did you have during the discussion? What went well?

5. Did you and your child come up with some house rules for dating? How do you plan to enforce those rules?

Parent–Child Discussion Starters

1. If your friend tells you that he and a girl are dating, what do you assume that means?

2. In your opinion, what are some benefits of building friendships with the opposite sex?

3. Check all that you agree with:

   ❏ Thirteen years old is a great age to start dating.

   ❏ It is not good for teen couples to spend every waking moment consumed with their relationship.

   ❏ In dating relationships, it's impossible to avoid making serious commitments.

4. What is the purpose of committing to be an exclusive couple, avoiding all other members of the opposite sex, when you are too young to pursue marriage?

5. TRUE or FALSE:

   Teenage committed relationships are often an exhausting roller coaster of relational ups and downs.

   _____

   Young people rarely neglect their family relationships and friendships once a boyfriend or girlfriend comes along.

   _____

6. What are your top priorities that you want to maintain, even if you are involved in a dating relationship?

7. In your opinion, why might it be necessary to guard your heart in a dating relationship (versus just guarding your body)?

8. Would you date someone who is not a Christian? Why or why not?

9. What do you think are some characteristics of an unhealthy dating relationship?

10. If you invite a member of the opposite sex to your house, what do you think the fair house rules would be?

Discussion Roadmap

1. **If your friend tells you that he and a girl are dating, what do you assume that to mean?**

    a. Understand what your child considers a dating relationship to be.

    b. Dating, in its simplest form, refers to a man and a woman getting to know each other (see page 170).

    c. The pivotal factor is the *degree* that we choose to get to know a member of the opposite sex (see page 170).

    d. Explain that the more intimate our premarital relationships are, the more of ourselves we give away (see page 170).

2. **In your opinion, what are some benefits of building friendships with the opposite sex?**

    a. Listen and respond to your child's ideas.

    b. Explain that there are benefits to getting acquainted with the opposite sex (see page 170).

    c. The key to dating is balance (see page 171).

    d. Discuss the ways that society's dating trends are out of balance (see page 171).

3. **Check all that you agree with:**

    ❑ **Thirteen years old is a great age to start dating.**

    a. "Do not stir up nor awaken love until it pleases" (Song of Sol. 2:7).

    b. Young teens are not mature enough to handle the pressures of dating (see page 172).

    c. Discuss these characteristics, which are ideal for teens entering the dating scene: responsible, decisive, trustworthy, obedient, spiritually astute, confident in personal convictions.

❑ **It is not good for teen couples to spend every moment consumed with their relationship.**

a. Discuss your child's answer.

b. Talk about the potential pitfalls (see page 173).

❑ **In dating relationships, it's impossible to avoid making serious commitments.**

a. Explain that we don't have to pursue deep levels of emotional and physical connection simply because that's the expectation and norm these days (see page 173).

b. Based on arguments provided throughout this chapter, discuss some reasons why dating relationships are the most advantageous when kept casual (see page 176).

4. **What is the purpose of committing to be an exclusive couple, avoiding all other members of the opposite sex, when you are too young to pursue marriage?**

a. These kinds of "forsake all other" commitments most often result when teen couples become so involved that they can't tolerate the idea of seeing their "honey" interested in anyone else (see page 174).

b. Discuss the problems (aka drama) that might result (see page 174).

c. Our kids shouldn't isolate themselves from the opposite sex, but they don't need to fill up their lives with them either (see page 175).

d. Discuss the difference between cultivating a friendship as opposed to a serious relationship (see page 175).

5. TRUE or FALSE:

   a. **Teenage committed relationships are often an exhausting roller coaster of relational ups and downs.**

   TRUE: Discuss how teen relationships suffer from being in "limbo" (see page 174).

   b. **Young people rarely neglect their family relationships and friendships once a boyfriend or girlfriend comes along.**

   FALSE: It is often the case that young people lose sight of key relationships and priorities as a result of having a boyfriend/girlfriend relationship (see page 175).

   Explain to your children that it is your responsibility, as a parent, to set boundaries that keep them balanced and on track with their priorities (see page 176).

6. **What are your top priorities that you want to maintain even if you are involved in a dating relationship?**

   a. Discuss your children's priorities; affirm any wise choices they have made; gently point out any unwise priorities they may have listed.

   b. Use this list to express any concerns you may currently have about your child's over-involvement in a dating relationship, or keep the list as a guide should a "love interest" come along.

   c. Discuss the benefits of maintaining friendships and the potential consequences of abandoning them for a member of the opposite sex (see page 176).

7. **In your opinion, why might it be necessary to guard your heart in a dating relationship (versus just guarding your body)?**

   a. "Keep [guard] your heart with all diligence, for out of it spring the issues of life" (Prov. 4:23).

b. The Bible tells us where our issues come from—the heart (mind, will, and emotions), which is why we have to diligently protect it (see page 176).

c. Discuss the regret young people experience, after breaking-up, if they have made strong emotional bonds (see page 177).

d. Stress that emotional intimacy leads to heightened physical temptation (see page 177).

e. Explain what "soul-ties" are (see page 177).

f. Abstinence is just as much about saving our hearts for our future mates as it is about saving our bodies (see page 177).

g. Just as we can't un-ring a bell, we can't undo emotional intimacy (see page 178).

8. **Would you date someone who is not a Christian? Why or why not?**

a. "Do not be unequally yoked together with unbelievers" (2 Cor. 6:14).

b. Dating someone in an effort to somehow modify his or her behavior is often referred to as "missionary dating" (see page 178).

c. Based on Second Corinthians 6:14, explain the fallacy of believing that God is calling a Christian to date a person in order to influence his/her spiritual beliefs and win him/her to the Lord (see page 178).

d. Missionary daters suffer from false guilt, erroneously concluding that the other person's well-being, future, and perhaps eternal destination, are dependent on the Christian's own ability to love, care, and transform that person (see page 179).

e. We don't need to "help God" by attempting to rescue members of the opposite sex through the avenue of dating relationships (see page 179).

f. Using the stool illustration, drive home the point
that, if someone is not healthy spiritually and emotionally, they should end the dating relationship
immediately (see page 179).

9. **What do you think are some characteristics of an unhealthy dating relationship?**

a. Read Hebrews 13: 4, followed by the story on page
180.

b. Go over the points in the Relationship Self Test (see
pages 183-185).

c. Perhaps you want to share some of the "Pointers
For Parents" so that your child knows what steps
you are going to take during the dating years.

10. **If you invite a member of the opposite sex to your
house, what do you think the fair house rules would be?**

Take this time to write out some house rules. Keep the list and
follow the boundaries defined on it.

In Summary

☆ Discuss the statements and statistics that are highlighted
in boxes throughout the chapter.

☆ Ask your child, "Do you have any questions about what
we've discussed today?"

THIRD STEP:

Motivation

Preparation

+

Application

+

Motivation

=

Inspiration

It's one thing to obtain a goal; it's quite another to maintain it.

Every January I encounter the same challenge at our local fitness center; it's a fight to procure a treadmill. The gym is full of new people, all having made the same New Year's resolution: "This year, I vow to exercise!" As a result, there's a crowd of unfamiliar faces prowling through the gym's cardio section, looking to pounce on the first treadmill relinquished by a weary runner.

By February, it's not nearly as difficult to find an open treadmill and by March, the gym is back to its normal capacity and there are plenty of treadmills to choose from. The reason? Most of the "New

Year's folks" lack the motivation to persevere in their resolution. Sure, they go through the trouble and expense of joining a gym. They even work out for a while. What they underestimate, however, is the long-term commitment, sacrifice, and effort it takes to *maintain* their goal.

I can't be too quick to point a critical finger at the fitness center "drop-outs" seeing as I personally have failed to follow through with my New Year's resolution for four consecutive years now—I'm going to keep up with my loved one's birthdays and mail out cards each month. Unfortunately my good intentions get swallowed up by old habits and complacency, and none of my out-of-town relatives with a birthday later than February get a card.

When it comes to our kids' decision to practice abstinence, they need a level of motivation that compels them to persevere through the years. This kind of enduring motivation is derived out of intense passion and conviction. The previous section of this book was designed to ignite those qualities in our kids while this section is geared to fan the flames of their passion and conviction so that their commitment to abstinence remains strong over the long haul. This is accomplished by:

☆ Providing our kids with solid answers to their uncertainties about abstinence so that they do not second guess their stance later.

☆ Alleviating fears our kids may have about somehow marrying the wrong person, which undermines their determination to wait for "the one."

☆ Extending powerful truths that lead our kids toward healing and freedom from past mistakes, regrets, and guilt.

☆ Expounding on the crucial elements that ultimately "make or break" one's ability to successfully remain abstinent until marriage.

I'm sure you've heard the cliché, *save the best for last!* That is truly what I have done in this book. The final chapter of this study contains the single most important point that we must communicate to our kids.

WHERE ARE THE TOOLS?

While you will still find **Questions for Thought**, I did not include any **Parent-Child Discussion Starter** questions for the remaining chapters because it is my desire that, moving forward, you practice the process of orchestrating the dialogue between you and your child. Based on the approach we took in the previous section, why not read through the following chapters and try developing your own list of thought-provoking questions? I encourage you to make your own **Discussion Roadmaps** as well. In this way, you become equipped to continue the discussion-based discipleship process with your child long after you have completed this study.

For those who, for whatever reason, are not able to develop their own **Parent-Child Discussion Starter** questions and **Discussion Roadmaps**, I have provided discussion questions and roadmaps for the following chapters on the Inspiring Abstinence website. Log onto www.InspiringAbstinence.com and click on the Parent tab. From there you can download the materials.

There is a wealth of spiritually edifying material available that we can study with our children using the simple, yet powerful, Q and A technique modeled in this book. As a matter of fact, this same approach works wonderfully as we read and discuss the Bible with our kids.

OBJECTIONS

Responding to Objections and Myths About Abstinence

Based on years of working with teenagers and listening to their uncertainties and misconceptions concerning abstinence, I have provided here the most common objections to abstinence, followed by solid rebuttals.[1]

It doesn't bother me when kids attempt to undermine the principles of abstinence because those tend to be the same kids who, in the long run, become the most passionate about remaining abstinent once the fallacy of their wrong thinking is lovingly exposed.

Let's not get angry or impatient if our kids question the validity of abstinence or do not quickly embrace it. Instead, let's thank God that we are blessed with children who are not easily swayed, knowing that this character quality can actually equate a strong commitment to godly convictions in their future. Nothing good comes from shutting down communication due to differences of opinions with our kids. Furthermore, they should have the liberty to express ideas that are different from ours. If they are thinking it, why not invite them to talk about it?

The beauty of God's Word is that His wisdom supersedes worldly philosophies and is well able to stand up to any "naysayer" or skeptic's criticism. Instead of forcing our kids to think as we do (as if that's even possible), let's *lead* them into realizations of truth through engaging conversations and ongoing discipleship.

MYTHS ABOUT ABSTINENCE

The following rebuttals are based primarily on simple logic versus spiritual understanding due to the fact that anyone who asserts such claims is failing to discern the spiritual implications of sex in the first place. As a result, these answers by themselves are insufficient—if we really want to inspire young people to abstinence we absolutely have to lead them to an understanding of the spiritual aspects of human sexuality as described throughout the Bible and in this text. However, I have found that it is beneficial to share these "common sense" arguments with young people because it helps to expose the shortcomings and pitfalls of worldly philosophies. It also helps build confidence in spiritually-minded kids who have already decided on premarital abstinence by reinforcing the wisdom of their decision and reminding them that God's ways are superior to the ways of humankind.

Myth #1: I don't want to marry someone until I know if we're sexually compatible.

Sex is an integral part of any marriage, but it is *not* the most important thing. Furthermore, there are many other factors besides sex that determine long-term compatibly with a spouse, such as spiritual maturity, family ideology, lifetime aspirations, and common social and recreational interests—just to name a few. It's not every day that we meet someone who is compatible in these crucial areas. Does it make any sense that, upon finding a unique love match based on these vitally important factors, we would then dump that person because we feel they could have performed better in bed?

Does it make any sense that, upon finding a unique love match, we would then dump that person because we feel they could have performed better in bed?

Of course we all want to have exciting sex lives with our spouses, but research proves that most couples actually have to work at their sexual compatibility, versus having some innate chemistry that keeps their sexual connection steamy and passionate over the years. Believe it or not, it was my grandmother who once told me, "There are worse things than sex to have to practice over and over until you get it just right." You know, she makes a valid point!

We don't need to physically try someone out to decide if we want to spend the rest of our lives with him or her. If our spiritual and emotional connections are there, and if we possess a strong sense of attraction toward that special someone, then we can rest assured that the physical connection will be there too once we're married (even if we have to practice a bit)!

Myth #2 – I need to be sexually experienced so I'll know how to satisfy my spouse someday.

While all women have the same reproductive anatomy, as do men, each individual has different preferences when it comes to physical touch and lovemaking. As a result, we have no business "learning" how to please our mates from anyone *but our mates*. Furthermore, I would hardly be impressed if my husband caressed me a certain way because that's how his ex-girlfriend liked to be touched!

It's beneficial to share the following contrasting scenarios with young people to expose the fallacy of becoming sexually experienced before marriage. Simply ask, "If your future mate was somehow able to contact you right now and have a short conversation with you, which would you rather hear her (or him) say?"

ONE: "Oh sweetheart! I can't wait to meet you! In the meantime, you'll be glad to know that I've been doing all kinds of sexual acts and favors for my boyfriend. This way I'll be prepared to seduce and satisfy you someday. He's teaching me a variety of useful techniques. I'll know exactly how to please you when we get married because I've been pleasing guys for years!"

TWO: "Oh sweetheart! I can't wait to meet you! In the meantime, I've been focusing my attention on Christ and growing in spiritual wisdom and maturity. There have been times I have been tempted to give my heart and body to someone else, but I chose not to because I sincerely believe you are worth waiting for. It's not always easy to wait, but I know it will all be worth it when you and I give ourselves to each other as husband and wife."

Conclusion: there's absolutely nothing romantic or impressive about becoming sexually experienced in preparation to please one's future spouse.

Myth #3 – It's OK to have sex as long I am engaged or planning to marry the person someday.

Would you let someone operate on you who says he plans to be a doctor in the future? How about if he just got accepted into medical school—would that provide enough creditability for you to allow him to remove your appendix? Of course not! We know that, until a person walks across the stage, receives his or her diploma, and officially graduates from medical school with a doctorate, he or she is no doctor!

Over 50 percent of teens ages 15-17 believed they would marry their first sexual partner.[2]

And so it is with marriage. Hoping to get married, making plans to get married, even wearing an engagement ring as a promise of getting married someday is not the same thing as *being* married. Furthermore, *intending* on committing to someone for life is not equivalent to *having* committed to someone for life.

For young people who insist that there's nothing wrong with having sex with someone as long as they plan to marry the person, here is a fun and effective assignment that you can give them to help expose the error of their thinking. Have them ask ten adults, "In your past, was there ever anyone you sincerely believed you would marry and perhaps even became engaged to, but you didn't end up marrying that person after all?" Almost every grownup has a story about a person they thought for sure they would marry, but the relationship actually never progressed to that point. Many people have testimonies of going as far as getting engaged to someone, only to break-up with their fiancée and forego marriage for one reason or another.

The conclusion is obvious—planning to marry someone can't possibly be the factor that makes sex OK because there is no way to know if we really will marry someone until we are, in fact, married.

Myth #4 – It's not realistic to wait until I'm married to have sex.

In today's society, teenagers often wonder if it is possible to be in their 20s, much less 30s or 40s, and still be a virgin. They worry, *What if I don't get married until I'm 35 and I have to stay a virgin until then?*

Ninety-two percent of teens reported that they think being a virgin in high school is a good thing.[3]

It's no wonder young people feel this way. In the last decade, Hollywood has released several blockbuster movies that derive their plot from making fun of a virgin. Until he has illicit intercourse at the conclusion of the movie, he is the subject of ridicule, humiliation, and scorn. More than one of these movies involves high school students striving to lose their virginity before graduation. Such films lead students to believe that they are social outcasts and failures if they don't "score" in their teens. What a cruel lie!

The truth is, it's actually unrealistic *not* to wait until we're married to start having sex! Allow me to explain.

Our physical bodies have three primary appetites: eating, sleeping, and having sex. All three of these appetites have something in common—they are insatiable, meaning that we cannot satisfy them once and for all. Think about it. No matter how much we eat today or how full we get, tomorrow we will get hungry all over again. And no matter how much sleep we get tonight, tomorrow night our bodies will be weary and ready to sleep again. And so it is with sex. Just because we have sex once doesn't mean we don't want to have sex again, and therein lies the problem.

When young people start having sex with a girlfriend or boyfriend, they regularly satisfy their sexual appetites. But what happens when they break-up? Who is going to satisfy their sexual cravings then? Are they just going to look for someone willing to have sex? Oftentimes the answer to this question is "yes," creating a destructive lifestyle of promiscuity.

> The man who has sexual relations on a feast-or-famine schedule...often develops a congested prostate during the famine periods. When he has frequent intercourse, the prostate produces seminal fluid to keep the pace. But when the sexual activity stops, the prostate is still working at the same rate to produce fluid, and the resulting congestion sometimes causes prostatitis. This requires prescription medication and prostatic massage by his physician, placing an index finger into the rectum and applying firm pressure to the unusually swollen and tender prostate gland.[4]

Unlike eating and sleeping, we don't *have to* engage our sexual appetites. Sure, we'll deal with ongoing cravings, but the moment we intentionally feed that appetite through sexual activity, those cravings escalate into desperate desires! Why not keep our sexual appetites under wraps until marriage, at which point we can have sex as often as we wish for the most part? Whereas sex outside of marriage leaves a person vulnerable to "feast or famine" sexual encounters, marriage is basically a feast for life!

Suppose we are not going to meet and marry our mate until we are 35 years old. Then why start having sex at 17 years of age, or even 25 for that matter? Who is going to satisfy that appetite for the next 10 or 18 years? Better to "let it sleep" than to wake up your sexual appetite without a lifelong sexual partner.

Myth #5—Masturbation is a great way to satisfy one's sexual longings while remaining abstinent until marriage.

Masturbation is the decision to sexually stimulate ourselves. It requires that we experience the most physically intimate act two people can share (sexual gratification) all alone. The ironic thing about masturbation is that, though it promises to temporarily satisfy our sexual desires, it only intensifies our longing for sex. Like a drug addict, we eventually become enslaved to the thing that we originally believed would serve us and meet our perceived needs.

For the person who desires a sexually pure life free from the guilt, addiction, and tormenting lust accompanied by perversion, you want to stay away from masturbation for the following valid reasons:

A. Masturbation does not satisfy, but instead, intensifies our longings for sex.

Let's face it, while masturbating, one is hardly imagining fluffy bunny rabbits hopping through a field showered with wildflowers. No, one must entertain sexually graphic thoughts in order to produce sexual feelings. In conjuring up and meditating on such sexually illicit and stimulating images, we intensely turn up the heat on our sexual appetites, which only makes our sexual cravings all the worse. What's more, it becomes nearly impossible to look at some-one we find attractive without envisioning having sex with him or her. When our minds are dominated by lust, we are no longer able to see members of the opposite sex for who they are on the inside, which makes it nearly impossible to cultivate healthy relationships with them and quickly becomes a source of torment.

B. What is supposed to connect us intimately to another in-stead leaves us feeling utterly alone.

Immediately after masturbating, reality confronts us—we were not ravished by a lover; we merely stimulated ourselves. This sober realization leaves us emotionally unsatisfied by the experience, making us more desperate for sexual intimacy, which drives us right back to masturbation. What a vicious cycle!

Loneliness is like a cloud of depression that hovers over one's head, continually overshadowing the joy and contentment that we long for. It has been my experience, in counseling young people who are involved in masturbation, that they tend to battle extreme feelings of loneliness. This is no mystery to me. *You can't experience the most bonding physical act (sex) all by yourself without feeling utterly lonely as a result.* It's better to resist occasional sexual urges than to masturbate and evoke relentless feelings of loneliness.

C. Masturbation is addicting.

I remember how confused I was the first time a lady friend of mine confided in me that she caught her husband masturbating. I wondered, *Why would he masturbate when he could have **real** sex with his wife?* I have since learned that masturbation often becomes a relentless addiction, in some cases compelling people to masturbate several times in a single day!

Since masturbation is based on fantasy, not reality, and involves intense meditation, people often become addicted to the mental and emotional escape that accompanies the act. The sexual scenario they've created in their minds starts to replace reality, often causing such people to prefer masturbation over actual intercourse with their spouse. This "out of touch with reality" means of existence makes a person vulnerable to all kinds of rash behaviors, illogical decisions, and mental and emotional breakdowns. If they are married, their addiction stands as an intimacy barrier between their spouse and them, which causes the marriage to break down.

D. Masturbation is self-centered, which is the essence of sin.

Just as we discussed in Chapter Eight, all sin has its origin in self-centeredness. Sexual gratification was created to be *given to us* by someone else (i.e. their anatomy stimulates ours, resulting in sexual climax). By stimulating ourselves, we are taking an act that is meant to be a give-and-take experience between two people and reducing it to a self-motivated (self-centered) experience. What's more, we are imagining having sex with someone who is not our mate, and in this way, we are guilty of adultery and/or fornication (see Matt. 5:28).

Myth #6—I don't see any need to get married; I prefer to live with my significant other.

It troubles me to consider the number of people who are now choosing to forego marriage and live together. In 2003, 9.2 million men and women lived together in unmarried-partner households.[5]

Two primary reasons people choose to cohabitate are:

1. People consider marriage to be irrelevant.

Young people want to know, "Does a ring on my finger and a signed marriage license really matter?" In light of our nation's current divorce rate, many young people see marriage as a useless ritual, an old tradition that need not be practiced in the future. I must concede that, if one perceives marriage to be nothing more than an expensive wedding, exchange of rings, and a piece of paper filed with the county clerk, it does seem a bit ridiculous. However, *marriage is so much more than these things!* It is a lifetime covenant commitment to one person witnessed by God Himself.

Married people have lower mortality, are more satisfied with their sexual lives, and have higher wages and higher financial savings.[6]

As we've discussed in previous chapters, marriage is God's idea, not humankind's. We have incorporated traditions like garters and grooms' cakes, but let us not lose sight of the essence of marriage and its relevance—*two lives joined as one for life!* Building families without lifelong commitments is like building a house on the sand; it will never have the kind of stability and security that we, and our children, deserve and desire.

In many cases, young people are afraid of lifetime commitments because they have grown up amidst our nation's plague of divorce. They've seen how painful and costly divorces are, and they are leery of making themselves vulnerable to a marital split. They erroneously conclude that, by not getting married, they will not suffer the consequences of divorce. You and I know that this is not true. Anytime you share a life together with someone by cohabitating with him or her, break-ups are painful and costly. And when the only prerequisite for a couple staying together is that they are happy with each other, as is often the case with cohabitation, we know that it's just a matter of time before a split occurs—all long-term relationships entail "peaks and valleys" and require ongoing compromise, sacrifice, and perseverance in order to survive.

Consider the following:

In more recent years, a large proportion of young people began living together soon after the onset of dating, with little intention of remaining together permanently, and even less of getting married. Breaking up then becomes much more difficult than if couples had simply continued to date each other.[7]

Does a marriage license ensure a couple will stay together for life? No. However, *two people embracing a covenant commitment with one another and building their relationship on the principles in God's Word is quite a different matter.*

Couples who possess a fear of lifetime commitments are doomed from the start—quality relationships cannot exist on a foundation of fear, but rather, they require trust.

2. People assume their marriage will be stronger if they live together first.

Research clearly proves that this philosophy is false. Couples who live together before marrying have nearly an *80 percent higher divorce rate than* those who do not.[8] Furthermore, more than half of couples who cohabitate split up within five years.[9] That's not all. Studies show that:[10]

- ☆ Couples who had cohabited had less positive problem-solving behaviors and were, on average, less supportive of each other than those who had not cohabited.

- ☆ Couples who had cohabited before marriage had much higher rates of premarital violence than those who had not lived together. This premarital violence then leads to higher rates of marital violence, another factor related to divorce.

- ☆ Those who cohabit are generally more approving of divorce as a solution to marital problems.

- ☆ A propensity to cohabit soon after starting a romantic relationship leads to a pattern of instability. People who go through a series of de facto relationships are more likely to contract quick marriages, which are harder to remain faithful to.

- ☆ In the 1970s, about 60 percent of couples living together went on to marry their partner within three years. By the early 1990s, this figure dropped to about 35 percent.

WHY BUY THE COW?

You've probably heard the crude yet fundamentally sound cliché, "Why buy the cow when you can get the milk free?" The truth is, we have no business living with someone, giving him or her access to everything in our lives that is sacred, without a commitment that assures the individual will love, honor, and cherish us for life. And certainly *kids* deserve this level of security from their parents!

> [In cohabitating relationships] young children are more likely to be injured or killed by their mother's live-in boyfriend than in biological families. Girls, for their part, are at higher risk of being sexually abused.[11]

On the occasions when a person defends the validity of living with a partner instead of getting married, I challenge the person's stance by explaining, "I understand *you* approve of this lifestyle, but are you at all familiar with how our nation's *children* feel about it? I encourage you to go interview a dozen elementary-age children who are dealing with live-in boyfriends or the absence of one of their parents and see how they feel about casually committed relationships." Most people do not realize that currently in the United States, an estimated 40 percent of all children will live with their single mother (never married or divorced) and her boyfriend at some point before their 16th birthday.[12] With this in mind, shouldn't we consider *their* thoughts and feelings on the issue?

Truth be told, there's not a kid on this planet who wouldn't want his or her biological mom and dad committed to one another for life in a marriage relationship that provides a healthy, loving, stable family environment free from abuse, strife, and the fear of separation. Why would we *intentionally* rob our kids of this?

THE MOTIVATION BEHIND ONE'S OBJECTIONS

I've been in a variety of settings where I am defending abstinence amidst the protests of others. As a result, I've come to understand that there are typically two kinds of people who present rebuttals. Some people make objections simply because they do not agree with me and are sincerely searching for the truth of the matter. Others make objections in an attempt to prove that they are right and could care less about arriving at truth. With the latter, no matter how many reasonable points we make, this type of person will not be swayed because they have determined in their hearts not to be. Knowing this, we must keep the "root" issue in mind as we share the logical reasons behind abstinence with our kids—*it ultimately comes down to their desire to surrender to God's ways or keep doing things their way.* This is why spiritual maturity and biblical discipleship must be the driving force behind our efforts to inspire abstinence.

Questions for Thought

(Before discussing the material with your child):

1. How do you react when someone confronts and disagrees with your point of view? Do you respond in a godly productive way?

2. In your opinion, why is it important to share common sense arguments in favor of abstinence with your child?

3. Are you already aware of certain objections that your child has to abstinence? If so, how do you plan to address these particular reservations?

(After discussing the material with your child):

4. What challenges did you have during the discussion? What went well?

5. Did your child make a statement or ask a question that you were not prepared to answer? How might you get prepared so that you can provide a solid response in the near future?

13

MARRIAGE

Preparing a Child to Choose the Right Mate

Corresponds with Chapter Nine in "Why Wait?"

I may have never met you, but I can confidentially say that I know something about you. You have a tendency to rely on yourself instead of God. There is no need to marvel at my astute observation, nor to get defensive—it's true of every person. Like a toddler who insists on shouting "No Daddy, I can do it myself," it is our human nature to exert our independence, as if to somehow prove to our Creator that we have everything under control (yeah, right). Oh sure, we eventually cry out to God for His help, but it is usually after we find ourselves utterly overwhelmed and helpless to cope with a dire circumstance of some sort.

The call to Christianity is *not* one of self-reliance and personal empowerment (despite what some "trendy" preachers proclaim these days). Biblical Christianity is about dependence on God's Spirit to save us, guide us, help us, and give us the grace we need to live each day for Him. It is about esteeming God's will for our lives over our personal agenda and surrendering to His competent leadership.

So how do we prepare our kids to find the right mate? The same way we prepare them to make every other significant life decision—*we teach them to rely on the Holy Spirit's guidance.*

Consider the essential life truths contained in these Scriptures—"Trust in the Lord with all your heart and lean not on your own understanding. In all your ways acknowledge Him and He shall direct your paths" (Prov. 3:5-7). Let's look at how this passage applies to one's desire to find the right mate:

TRUST IN THE LORD WITH ALL YOUR HEART

Our kids can trust God with their future, including who they will marry. They can count on God to bring the right person at the right time into their lives for the purpose of marriage. Is God forgetful? Uninterested? Irresponsible? Not at all! While He can be unpredictable, He is faithful, and our kids can confidently put their trust in Him. They don't have to frantically search for love the way that unbelievers do, often basing the bulk of their marriage decision on physical attraction.

LEAN NOT ON YOUR OWN UNDERSTANDING

Everyone tends to be on their best behavior while on a date. In dating relationships, men don't usually lose their tempers, pass gas, or admit to having an addiction to pornography. Women rarely nag, cry for no reason, or confess their true motives—"I'm looking for a wealthy man who will marry me and buy me everything I want." The point is, we need the Holy Spirit to help us discern whether someone is or isn't the right mate for us, versus relying exclusively on our own impressions and feelings, which can be seriously misleading. Only God knows the true intent and condition of another person's heart, and we need to be sensitive to what He is telling us about someone we're interested in. God also speaks through people, so we should not ignore any "red flags" or concerns our friends or loved ones have about the person we're considering marrying.

In All of Your Ways Acknowledge Him

As previously discussed, we have a tendency to be self-reliant and to call on God only when we are suffering. It's amazing to think that the God of the universe is ready and willing to guide us in every situation but that we forego His help, preferring to face life in our own extremely limited strength and understanding. When it comes to finding a mate, we should include God in *every* aspect of that process—how we handle our feelings of attraction, who we enter into dating relationships with, what to look for in a mate, how to prepare for marriage, etc. We include Him by following the wisdom of His Word and asking Him to show us His will in all things. Our next point tells us what we can expect when we do this.

He Shall Direct Your Paths

When we trust God, depend on Him more than on our own limited understanding, and acknowledge Him in our desire to find a mate, He promises to direct *our paths*. Think about this—He not only directs us (see Rom. 8:14), but He directs our paths, which is to say, He dictates what comes our way. You and I cannot possibly control who will and won't cross our paths tomorrow, but God can! He can ensure that we meet the person who is to be our soul mate for life. That sounds like a much better proposition to me than going from one singles event to the next, exhausting myself looking for *Mr. Right!* I'd much rather rest in knowing that, as I serve God and pattern my life after the truths in His Word, He will make sure my future spouse and I find one another and recognize the need to be together.

Furthermore, we don't have to stress about figuring out who "the one" is. God does not hide His will from us so that we must anxiously search for clues as if we're solving some sort of mystery. His will simply unfolds as we serve Him daily and live in obedience.

DOES DATING VIOLATE THESE PRINCIPLES?

How does the concept of dating align with the wisdom found in Proverbs 3:6-7? If a young adult is cultivating a friendship with a member of the opposite sex while maintaining healthy boundaries and all the while honoring God in every aspect of the relationship, that's one thing. However, if our dating efforts are motivated by our own self-willed determination to find and secure a mate, we are setting ourselves up for disappointment.

No one drives off a car sales lot with a "lemon" on purpose—they test drive cars until they find the one they like best and are totally un-aware as they sign the loan papers that they have selected a vehicle plagued by malfunctions. And so it often is with dating. A self-willed young man dates one young lady after another in search of the "best one," only to find that the girl he eventually commits to is not the kind of person he assumed she was. While *every* marriage requires couples to work through differences and some unforeseen compatibility issues, this young man arrives at the tragic conclusion that he married some-one under false pretenses—she's not the kind of person she seemed to be while they dated. (The ironic thing is, he probably isn't either.)

If we're going to find a mate God's way, we can't pattern our premarital standards and behaviors after what we see our society doing. After all, the masses place very little trust in God (if any), tend to rely solely on their own understanding, and rarely acknowl-edge God in any area of their lives, and therefore, they do not walk on God-ordained paths.

Some young people choose to forego the traditional dating scene, preferring not to get involved as "more than friends" with members of the opposite sex while they prepare to meet the one whom God has set apart to be their mate. They choose to trust by faith that God will bring their future spouse across their paths at the right time, and He will clearly reveal who that person is. Is there any biblical precedence for this approach? Let's take a look.

AN OLD TESTAMENT ACCOUNT WITH A MODERN-DAY APPLICATION

All kids love a good story, and the Bible is chock full of them, especially the Old Testament. The following story is not only one of my kids' favorites, but it also contains profound principles about finding a mate that we can apply to our lives.

Instead of copying the passages directly out of the Bible, I will paraphrase the story (with accuracy), because this is the best way to portray biblical accounts to our kids (youngsters and teens)—not by reading them line by line but by reciting them from memory with expression, and eye contact. As you will see from my example, we can also have fun with the stories as well. This is the account of how Isaac and Rebekah met, recorded in the 24th chapter of Genesis:

Abraham was getting very old and was concerned that his son, Isaac, needed a wife. While sipping on a low-fat Starbucks frappuccino one morning (OK, a slight exaggeration), Abraham began worrying that Isaac would marry a local woman who did not worship God. So Abraham called on his trustworthy servant to travel to the town where they previously lived to find the ideal wife for Isaac since the women living there served God. Abraham's servant recognized that this was a very important task, and he asked Abraham, "What if the young woman I find will not move here from your old hometown? Should Isaac move there to be with her?"

"No!" Abraham insisted. "We are living where God told us to, and my son cannot disobey God in order to get married. We must stay in God's will by staying here." Abraham went on to tell his servant, "If you find the right woman for Isaac, but she is not willing to come back here with you to live with us, then just come home without her—I won't blame you."

But the servant was worried, "What if I can't figure out which woman to choose?" Abraham explained that an angel would go to the city before him and give him a sign so that he would know which woman was the right one for Isaac. So the servant vowed to do as Abraham asked and loaded up several camels for the journey. He packed gifts to give the special woman and her family once he found her, including an insulated Starbucks travel mug (you never know).

He traveled to Abraham's hometown and arrived one evening, just as the women were heading down to the well to draw water. The servant humbly prayed, "Oh Lord, give me success and show kindness to Abraham by showing me which woman to choose for Isaac. This is my request—I will ask one of them for a drink, and if she says yes, and offers water for my camels too, I will know that she is the one! Thank you for your kindness, Lord."

As he was still praying, a young woman named Rebekah arrived with a water jug on her shoulder. She was a beautiful lady who was saving herself for her husband and had never been intimate with a man. The servant spotted her, ran over to her, and asked, "May I have a drink?"

"Certainly, sir!" Rebekah kindly said and gave him a grande caramel latte with a double shot of espresso. OK, she actually gave him some water. She then offered to provide water for his camels, which appeared to be an answer to the servant's prayers! As she generously provided water for his camels, the servant watched her and prayed, "Lord, is this really the one?" He soon felt convinced that Rebekah *was* the one, so he gave her all kinds of costly jewelry and gifts and asked to meet her parents. He was so grateful that the Lord had answered his prayer, and when Rebekah agreed to take him to meet her parents, he fell to his knees and thanked the Lord!

Rebekah's family was very nice. The servant explained why he was there and that he hoped to bring Rebekah home to meet and marry Isaac. Rebekah's parents realized that it was God's will that she leave their home and get married, but they were hesitant to see her go. They were sad that their daughter was leaving, but Rebekah assured them she was ready. The servant gave gifts to her parents (they absolutely loved the Starbucks mug!) and then left with Rebekah to take her to meet Isaac and his coffee drinking family.

Meanwhile Isaac was taking a walk in a field and prayerfully thinking about things. Suddenly he looked up and saw the camels coming. When Rebekah saw Isaac, she noticed him from far off and wanted to know who he was. The servant explained that he was Isaac, the man she was to marry. Isaac and Rebekah met and married, and Isaac loved his wife very much! She was a special comfort to him after his mother died.

Isaac and Rebekah went on to have children together, and their children had children, and so on and so on until finally Jesus Christ was born through their descendants!

WHAT CAN WE LEARN FROM ISAAC AND REBEKAH'S STORY?

Now please don't panic and think I'm about to suggest that your child have an arranged marriage! I simply want to highlight some of the spiritual principles evident in this historical account.

1. Abraham was concerned that Isaac needed a wife.

In this story, we can view Abraham as a type (representation) of God the Father. Just as Abraham was aware that it was time for Isaac to get married, God also knows when we are ready for marriage. He *is* concerned with when and whom we marry.

2. Abraham was worried that Isaac would marry a woman who did not worship God.

We are commanded in Scripture not to marry an unbeliever (see 2 Cor. 6:14). It is very difficult to serve God when our mate objects to our faith, or simply chooses not to serve God alongside us. And how confusing it is for kids to have parents who don't agree on who God is!

3. Abraham called on his trustworthy servant to find the ideal wife for Isaac.

The servant can be viewed as a type (representation) of the Holy Spirit, who is at work in the earth today. When God the Father decides it's time for us to get married, the Holy Spirit leads us to that person. We don't have to stress about finding a mate.

4. Abraham would not allow his son to disobey God in order to get married.

If God has called us to live in a certain place, serve in a specific ministry, or fulfill a particular assignment in the Body of Christ, we shouldn't neglect that to get married. For example, if a man is called to the mission field but a woman asks him to give up mission work to marry her, she's not the right one for him. Certainly our assignments from God change over the years, and the missionary may eventually be called to stay home, but this must be according to God's plan, not an attempt to satisfy someone else's plan.

5. Abraham said, "If you find the right woman for Isaac, but she is not willing, come home without her."

Even if it's God's will that two people be joined together in marriage, He does not force this on them. Marriage is always the result of each person's free will decision. Sometimes a Christian will feel confident that he has found the one he is to marry, but the girl he's set his sights on does not reciprocate such feelings. In such cases, we would never want to insist that someone marry us based on what "God showed us." The person God has for us will *want* to be with us as much as we want to be with him or her.

6. The servant knew which woman was the right one for Isaac.

The Holy Spirit knows which person is right for us. As previously stated, we can trust God to bring a suitable mate into our lives. We don't have to exhaust ourselves trying to make something happen at the wrong time or with the wrong person.

7. Rebekah was a beautiful lady who was saving herself for her husband and had never been intimate with a man.

There are two things to point out here. First, it's no coincidence that the servant/Holy Spirit noticed the one who was saving herself for her husband. This gesture of faith and obedience to God gets His attention! Also, beauty and premarital virginity are always linked together in the Bible. A woman of virtue has an attraction that supersedes physical beauty.

8. The helper asked to meet Rebekah's parents.

As parents, the Holy Spirit will often give us peace or a sense of concern about someone our kids are dating or considering marrying. Young people do a great disservice to themselves if they ignore any concerns their parents may have about a potential spouse since God often leads us through our parents' discernment.

9. Rebekah's parents realized it was God's will that she leave their home and get married, but they were hesitant to see her go.

When God brings your child together with his or her future mate, the couple deserves your blessing. By letting our kids "leave our home," we release them to live with their spouse free of our nosy or overbearing interference in their relationship.

10. Rebekah assured her parents that she was ready[to get married].

We have to be careful as parents that we don't push our kids toward marrying a certain person just because we believe we've found the ideal mate for them. The day will come when our kids are ready to pursue marriage *when and with whom* they choose. We don't want to manipulate or force something on our kids that they don't truly desire for themselves (I've seen it happen on several occasions, and it always ends in devastation).

11. The servant gave gifts to her parents.

What a *gift* from God it is when the Holy Spirit leads our kids to godly spouses! Let us always treat our sons-in-law and/or daughters-in-law as the gifts they are and thank God for blessing us with them. Besides, they will most likely provide us with grandbabies— the best gift of all!

12. Isaac was taking a walk in a field and prayerfully thinking about things.

Notice what Isaac *wasn't* doing. He wasn't making out with another girl! He also wasn't pacing back and forth worried that God would somehow drop the ball and fail to bring him a suitable wife. He was at peace, trusting that the servant/Holy Spirit would bring his wife to him according to His own perfect plan.

13. When Rebekah saw Isaac, she noticed him and wanted to know who he was.

Young people often express their concern, "What if I'm not attracted to the person God picks to be my spouse?" My traditional reply—"Then God isn't very bright, is He?" Of course God knows attraction is a necessary part of a marriage relationship, and certainly, in His all-knowing nature, He is plenty wise enough to pick a mate for us that we will find attractive. (I don't care how godly someone is or how well you two get along; if you aren't attracted to him or her, don't get married!)

14. Isaac and Rebekah went on to have children together, and their children had children, and so on and so on until finally Jesus Christ was born through their descendants!

Our union with our spouse is always about the bigger picture— God's purpose in the earth. While we do enjoy companionship and intimacy with our spouse, God is working to accomplish something more significant than our own fulfillment. As we rear godly offspring, serve God alongside each other, and determine to help our mates accomplish all that God is calling them to, our relationship becomes *eternally* significant. As a result, we can leave a legacy that influences our family and others for generations to come!

How Will I Know When I've Found My Future Spouse?

Modern pregnancy tests make it easy for women to get an answer to the question, "Am I pregnant?" Two lines—*yes*. One line—*no*. That's virtually all there is to it. If only there were a test that provided a concrete yes or no to the question, "Should I marry this person?" While there is no such litmus test, there actually is a way to know with confidence whether we should marry someone. *We can hear from God.*

In 1960, only 13 percent of all teenage mothers in the Unites States were unmarried, compared with 81 percent in 2003.[1]

We don't hear from God the same way we hear from people, with our physical ears. We listen to the voice of God with our spiritual ears. That's why Jesus so often said, "Let him who has ears to hear, hear what the Spirit is saying" (see Rev. 2:11).

Did you know that you have spiritual ears? The Lord is continually speaking to us by His Spirit, but we don't always recognize His voice. To learn more about how to hear God, I recommend Peter Lord's book, appropriately named, *Hearing God*.[2] It is a tremendous resource and training tool for developing our spiritual sense of hearing.

In addition to speaking to us by His Spirit, God also reveals His will to us through His Word, through confirming circumstances, and through people (godly counsel). If all of these avenues are pointing to a "yes," we can trust that we have entered into God's will and proceed with marriage without fear of having missed the mark.

Mom or Dad, how can we help our kids choose the right mates? *We can teach them to ask God for direction and to obey what He tells them.* Consider the offer God extends to us in James 1:5—if we lack wisdom, we can ask God what we should do, and He will not frown upon our uncertainty, but will instead gladly answer us.

Do our children know that they can ask God questions and bring inquiries to God in prayer? Do they realize God that has promised to answer their questions and show them what to do?

Let's teach our kids to rely on God and to submit their life decisions, especially whom they will marry, to His counsel. As we model a lifestyle of hearing from God ourselves, and encourage them to do the same, they can choose their mates with confidence because they have become familiar with hearing and heeding God's voice and recognizing the ways God confirms His will in our lives.

Learning to discern God's will has lifetime benefits that go beyond choosing the right mate. The Christian life is meant to be lived with a daily assurance that we are smack-dab in the middle of God's perfect will for our lives; this brings the confidence and peace of mind that we need in order to endure trying seasons of tribulation and trial.

What a tragedy it is to marry someone under the impression that he or she is a Christian, only to find that individual uncommitted to prayer, biblical standards, Spirit-led living, or Christ-like love.

Don't Make This Mistake

A single person's desire to find a future mate is accompanied by everyday interactions with members of the opposite sex. At times, the single will form attractions toward a certain someone and wonder if there's any potential for a "love match." It is at this point that some Christians make a serious mistake. We know our future mate needs to be a Christian, so we simply ask the person we're interested in, "Are you a Christian?"

"Why yes, I am," the person quickly responds. We take this profession of Christianity at face value and make premature assumptions about his or her spirituality. It's as if we simply check the "Christian box" on our list of marital prerequisites with hardly enough objectivity.

Anyone can say he is a Christian. As a matter of fact, nationwide polls indicate that over 80 percent of Americans profess to be Christians. Why do we teach evolution instead of Intelligent Design in our public schools if the large majority of our country identifies with the God of the Bible? The answer is simple—there are lots of people naming the name of Christ who, in actuality, do not know or serve Him. They may own a Bible and even attend church, but like my husband always says, "Sitting in church doesn't make you a Christian any more than sitting in McDonalds makes you a Happy Meal!"

We can't know if someone is a Christian until we have time to observe the way that he or she lives. It's not that we arrogantly evaluate a person's Christian performance; it's that we look for evidence that points to a sincere versus shallow commitment to Christ. What a tragedy it is to marry someone under the impression that he or she is a Christian, only to find that individual uncommitted to prayer, biblical standards, Spirit-led living, or Christ-like love.

DON'T MAKE THESE MISTAKES EITHER

Here are some additional mistakes that singles often make. Let's warn our kids about these!

Second marriages end in divorce more often than first marriages, with each divorce stressful on both adults and children.[3]

1. Don't ignore others concerns.

To reiterate a point previously made, we often ignore our parents' and friends' warnings and honest concerns about our dating relationships. If the people who love us have a "bad feeling" about someone we're involved with, we should take their reservations to heart and give careful consideration to the validity of their concerns, versus merely defending the relationship. Too often, young people marry someone despite their loved one's warnings only to find out that their family and friends were right about the person all along.

2. Don't confuse your emotions with the Holy Spirit.

Don't misinterpret strong emotions as the Holy Spirit's leading. Even in the midst of the goose bumps, hot flashes, sweaty palms, and butterflies that accompany feelings of attraction and adoration, the Holy Spirit may be shouting "No, she's not the one!" We need to be careful to discern the difference between our emotions and what God is truly telling us.

3. Don't read too much into so-called "signs" from God.

Beware of bogus signs from God. Young people often assume ironic or "mystical" experiences are an indication that God has ordained a certain relationship when in reality, this is not the case. For example, a girl once told me, "I know I'm supposed to marry this guy because the first time he called me on the phone, the song, 'You're the One,' came on the radio!" A young man shared with me, "I know my girlfriend is my soul-mate for life because her middle name is the same as my mother's, and she passed away when I was two." That girl very well may be his soul-mate for life but it's not because she shares his mother's name. Remember, we're to be led by the Spirit of God, not by coincidences or unrelated signs.

Teenage fathers tend to have limited financial resources, poor academic performance, and high dropout rates.[4]

4. Don't marry out of desperation.

Out of desperation, many people marry the first person who takes an interest in them even though the relationship is somewhat lacking in chemistry and companionship. Out of fear that they may never meet or attract someone they really respect, they settle for a mediocre relationship. Not a good idea!

5. Don't overlook significant shortcomings.

Don't overlook someone's extreme shortcomings just because you are anxious to be married. Marriage is far too serious of a commitment to make as a result of impatience. Take an objective look at the person you're with, and don't be in denial about his or her flawed character just because you don't like the idea of waiting on someone more suitable to come along. Better to marry the right person when we're 35 years old than the wrong person a decade sooner.

6. Don't assume your partner will change.

Whatever you do, don't assume someone is going to change just because you two get married! As a matter of fact, in marriage, people tend to become *more* of what they already are. If she's insecure now, she'll be even more insecure after marriage. If he loses his temper now, he'll be even *more* temperamental after saying *I do*. Yes, God can change people, but we can never afford to marry with the hope that people will change, because they often don't. It's a huge mistake! And in the long run, it's much easier to remain single and to find a more compatible person than to try changing someone after marriage.

UNREALISTIC EXPECTATIONS

I cannot close this chapter without stressing one final imperative point. Just because we maintain our virginity and marry the one God has for us does not mean that our marriage will be utter bliss all of the time! By its very nature, marriage is challenging. The reason we honor God with our love life—wait until we're married to have sex and marry the one He has for us—is because we love Him! The marital companionship we reap is the icing on the cake. Furthermore, the marital obstacles we encounter become divine opportunities to mature in persevering love.

Now that we've discussed issues surrounding the finding of a mate, let's look at how we can help our kids pick up the pieces if they've already lost their virginity or sexual innocence through premature sexual experiences.

Questions for Thought:

(Before discussing the material with your child):

1. Explain the difference between a lifestyle of self-reliance as opposed to a God-reliant life.

2. How do society's traditional methods for finding and securing a mate contrast with the instructions and promise provided to believers in Proverbs 3:6-7 ("Trust in the Lord with all your heart and lean not on your own understanding. In all your ways acknowledge Him and He will direct your paths.")?

3. What points stood out to you the most under the "What Can We Learn From Isaac and Rebekah's Story?" section of the chapter?

(After discussing the material with your child):

4. What challenges did you have during the discussion? What went well?

5. Do you or your child need to learn more about how to recognize God's voice and discern His will? If so, what resources do you plan to utilize?

RENEWAL

No Longer a Virgin?

Corresponds with Chapter Ten in "Why Wait?"

As previously stated, the principles in this book are just as applicable for parents whose children have already had a sexual relationship as it is for parents whose kids are still virgins. The reason I can make this claim is because *we serve a redeeming God*. He is an expert at rescuing us out of guilt, confusion, and shame and restoring honor, purpose, and purity to our lives.

If your child has already become sexually active, I have good news for you—*it's not too late to intervene*. The sexual pitfalls of your child's past can be the very springboard that propels him or her toward sexual purity in the future, not to mention a richer relationship with God.

Let's take a step-by-step look at the transformation process.

STEP ONE: RECONNECTION

Yesterday I listened in horror as a local news anchor explained that a 14-year-old girl gave birth to a baby in the restroom at her middle school and then proceeded to try and flush the infant down the toilet. Needless to say, the newborn died. As reporters interviewed parents around campus, one mother's assessment of the situation made me want to hurl my remote control right through the television screen. *"The school* needs to do something about these kinds of situations!"

The school? I could not believe my ears! What about the parents?

At least one-third of teenage parents are themselves products of adolescent pregnancy.[1]

Upon discovering our kids' sexual activity, we all have a tendency to point the finger at multiple sources, but the painful truth is that we must examine *ourselves.* As parents, we are the primary authorities and spiritual leaders in our kids' lives, and it is ultimately our responsibility if our kids have fallen prey to sexual temptation. While nothing good comes from wallowing in guilt, a tremendous amount of good will result from identifying where we missed the mark and acknowledging that we have failed. Based on the mandates presented throughout this book, let's take an honest look at how our actions (or lack thereof) left our children ill-prepared to overcome sexual temptation. Until we do this, we cannot begin the healing and reconnection process with our kids.

Once we come to some conclusions about where we have gone wrong, it's time to talk to our kids. More specifically, it's time to repent to our kids.

The Reality of Repentance

Repenting and saying we're sorry are two different things. When we tell someone we are sorry, we rightfully acknowledge our wrongdoing, but this is just half of the reconciliation process; it is only complete when the other person is given an opportunity to release the offense that he or she is holding against us. In other words, when we repent to our kids by asking, "Will you forgive me?" they are empowered to make a decision—"Am I going to forgive or hold onto my anger and hurt?"

Repenting and saying we're sorry are two different things.

It's just as essential for a person to release a grudge as it is for a guilty person to confess and repent of the offense. In our home, we don't just tell one another we're sorry. We repent by asking, "Will you forgive me"? What a beautiful sight it is to see my children reconcile with each other by saying, "Yes, I forgive you," followed by a loving hug.

It's important to teach our kids that *forgiveness is a decision*, not a feeling. They may still feel angry or wounded by what we have (or someone else has) done or said to them, but they can choose to release that grudge—not because what we did was OK, but because they cannot heal until they let go of bitterness. Simply put, we cannot clutch resentment and have open hands to receive God's healing at the same time. Also, it is irrational to expect God to forgive our sins when we are not willing to forgive others of their sins.

...be kind to one another, tenderhearted, forgiving one another, even as God in Christ forgave you (Ephesians 4:32).

Perhaps when we repent to our kids, they will attempt to assure us that it is not our fault that they chose to have sex. It is true that they are accountable for their decisions, and we will soon look at how repentance on their part is necessary. However, our kids must check off on the fact that we played a part in the situation; otherwise they will carry false guilt. Take time to explain to your child how your actions compromised his (or her) ability to avoid and resist sexual temptation. This will go a long way toward the healing process in his life.

Once you've acknowledged where things went wrong, start talking to your child about how you plan to make things right from that day on. Reconnect with your child in such a way that you and he are not destined to repeat the mistakes of the past. Moving forward, determine to keep communication open and honest and keep biblical discipleship as your top priority.

STEP TWO: REALIZATION

Chances are, if our children chose to have sex, they are not fully aware of the sacredness of sex, the reasons sex outside of marriage is sinful, or the benefits of waiting until marriage to become sexually active. We must help our kids to realize these truths by teaching them the principles covered in the previous chapters of this book.

In the United States, according to national surveys, 77 percent of young people have had sex by age 20.[2]

It is important to note that premarital sex and disobedience go hand-in-hand. Chances are our kids have lied, snuck around, and perhaps deliberately disobeyed us in order to pursue their physical relationship. However, there's no sense in coercing repentance from our children before they feel remorse over their actions. Furthermore, guilt trips only produce momentary guilt, not long-term convictions. Knowing this, don't angrily insist that children see "the error of their ways." Instead, roll up your sleeves and get busy teaching them God's principles about sex; allow the Holy Spirit to open their eyes to the spiritual implications of sexual intimacy and the seriousness of having disobeyed their parents. Once they grasp the full magnitude of their actions, they will be in a position to repent out of the sincerity of their heart. After all, *there is no real repentance without sincerity.*

STEP THREE: REPENTANCE

Biblical repentance is the act of turning away from a particular behavior with no intention of ever repeating that behavior. It is as if we do an "about-face" in some aspect of our lifestyle. Repentance is the method God has instituted to cleanse us from our sin and guilt (made possible only through the blood of Jesus) (see Eph. 1:7). Like forgiveness, repentance is a *decision,* not a mere emotion, though it usually involves emotions since it is characterized by authentic remorse.

While we do not want to force repentance on our kids, we *do* want to stress the importance of it and make sure they understand how to receive God's forgiveness. When we confess our sins to God and ask Him to forgive us based on the blood of Jesus, which covers our transgressions, God will release us from our sin and no longer hold it against us. We are also commanded to repent to those we've sinned against, which means our kids do need to repent to us for any disobedience associated with their sexual exploits.

In a national survey, more than half of teenage boys and girls reported having given or received oral sex.[3]

It sure would be nice if, upon repenting, an invoice dropped down from Heaven that said, "Your sin is officially forgiven; signed, God." Instead we must receive forgiveness by faith, trusting that God has released us from guilt based on His Word and Christ's sacrifice. It is only after our kids have repented for their sexual sins and received God's forgiveness by faith that they are in a position for restoration.

STEP FOUR: RESTORATION

When I was about 8 years old, I used to love to go play at my best friend Julie's house. One day in particular, we were running through the living room and Julie accidentally slammed into a coffee table, knocking one of her mother's vases to the floor. The loud crash immediately silenced our giggles. We stared wide-eyed at the broken pieces and wondered how in the world we were going to avoid serious punishment. The solution was obvious—we had to glue that vase back together before Julie's mom saw it! We got out the super-glue and carefully patched the colorful vase back together.

By the time the glue dried, we were quite relieved. You could only tell the vase had been repaired if you looked closely at it. We put it back on the coffee table, only now the vase was nestled behind an artificial plant to disguise the cracks. Our hope was that Julie's mom wouldn't pay close attention to her beloved vase. (Did I mention that it was an heirloom?) Having saved the day with our "brilliant" restoration efforts, Julie and I went back to playing and forgot all about the ordeal. (I wonder if she ever got caught and disciplined for that?)

> **The most common STD is human papilloma virus (HPV), which sometimes produces warts on the genitals. It is the leading cause of cervical cancer in women.[4]**

For many years, this was my understanding of God's restoration—He takes the broken pieces of my life (my hurts, sins, and mistakes) and patches them back together to make me look as if everything is fine. As long as I keep a safe distance from others and don't allow them to get too close, they won't notice how fragile and broken I really am.

I have since learned that God's restoration is not about disguising our brokenness, but rather, about totally healing it. What if Julie and I could have taken that broken vase to the artist who created it? And what if that artist then took those broken pieces, melted, molded, and reset the shape of the vase and then reapplied the decorative artwork by hand? When he was done, there would be no cracks or broken pieces, only a beautiful masterpiece that need not be disguised or hidden.

> **For I will restore health to you and heal you of your wounds, says the Lord (Jeremiah 30:17).**

Restoration in our kids' lives is not about covering up what they did or masking the hurts they acquired; it's about getting totally healed. Their experiences with premature sex may have left our kids feeling like "used goods" or under–valued people. Then again, maybe they feel guilty for having been the initiator in the sexual relationship. No matter the case, our kids need to know that God, their loving Creator, wants to restore the way they see themselves.

There is no magic formula for bringing about this restoration. It simply comes as a result of desiring to know God more and receiving His healing touch. The more we learn who God is, the more He shows us who we are and, equally important, who we are *not.* As our kids relate to God through reading His Word and enjoying open and honest discussions about Him and with Him, God will heal their wounds and redefine how they view themselves. Our kids need not cover up their shortcomings before entering into prayer. On the contrary, they should release their hurts, disappointments, and failures into His competent hands. Parents, we must covey these healing truths to our kids.

STEP FIVE: RENEWAL

Our kids will know that they've entered into renewal when they no longer identify with the hurt and guilt associated with the sins of their past. While they likely will remember how the pain felt, they are no longer victims of that pain. In the renewal phase, it's not that our kids suddenly have it all together and can boast in their Christian performance; they are just more dependent than ever on the Holy Spirit to strengthen them to live the Christian life. Righteous living is a matter of will, but not willpower; the issue is *will* we surrender to the Spirit's leadership in our lives?

When we are enjoying a love relationship with Christ and are preoccupied with Him, we begin to lose sight of our selfish, carnal motivations. We don't have time to focus on our performance because we are so focused on serving the One who *is* perfect, Jesus Christ.

> **Teenage unwed mothers and their families are likely to suffer financially. Child support laws are spottily enforced, court-ordered payments are often inadequate, and many young fathers cannot afford them.**[5]

A natural byproduct of our kids having passed through reconnection, realization, repentance, and restoration and into the renewal phase of the transformation process is that they are now in a position to take their past mess-ups and turn them into encouraging messages! By this point, our kids have learned so much through their experiences and grown so significantly in their faith that they have a testimony that can inspire and impact their peers in a momentous way. The very traps and inflictions that the enemy intended to use to cripple our children in their walk with the Lord become the catalyst that inspires them to run their race with purpose and passion. As a result, their spiritual zeal becomes infectious to those around them.

Parents, let's prayerfully and patiently walk our kids through the transformation process, trusting that the Holy Spirit is at work in our children's hearts.

VIRGINITY: MORE THAN A PHYSICAL STATE

The last thing we want our kids thinking is that there's no point in abstaining from sex since they've already "blown it." As previously discussed, virginity is more than a physical state; it is a state of mind. It is a decision to wait until marriage to have sex based on the belief that there are spiritual implications to sex. While there is no way for our kids to reclaim their virginity once they have become sexually active, they can always make the decision to stop. At any time our kids can begin trusting God's plan and reserving their hearts and bodies for marriage.

We must be the loving voice of reason in our kids' lives that reminds them they *do* have a choice.

Questions for Thought

(Before discussing the material with your child):

1. In what ways have you failed to safeguard your child against sexual activity? In what ways are you going to do things differently in the future?

2. In your own words, explain the difference between saying sorry and repenting. Why is it important to repent versus just saying we're sorry?

3. What do you plan to say to your child to assure him or her that it is not too late to make a commitment to abstinence?

(After discussing the material with your child):

4. What challenges did you have during the discussion? What went well?

5. Based on the chapter's explanation of the five-step transformation process, what actions do you plan to take to help your child keep progressing through the steps?

LONG-TERM SUCCESS

Encouraging Abstinence Commitment

Corresponds with Chapter Eleven in "Why Wait?"

My husband and I were watching an intense college basketball game on television the other night, and while his eyes were glued to the players, I found myself observing the fans. Every time their home team made a basket, the cheerleaders, students, parents, and alumni jumped to their feet to applaud and cheer the boys' efforts. And when the opposing team scored on their beloved players, the fans offered up shouts of encouragement, "That's OK—we'll get em' back!" Even my husband passionately called out to his favorite team, as if the players and coaches could clearly hear his strategies and support from the privacy of our living room.

I couldn't help but wonder what that game would be like without the fans. What if the stadium was completely empty while the two teams battled it out on the court? I have a feeling both teams would still give a hearty effort. What would be missing, however, would be the ongoing encouragement, excitement, and support from the hometown fans. What's more, when the winning shot swooshed through the net, there would be no collective shout of triumph, no victory celebration—just the sound of the buzzer and weary players congratulating each other.

Parents, when our kids arrive at the conclusion that they want to wait until they are married to have sex, we need to celebrate! Just as fans rejoice in their teams' victories, our kids need to see us get excited about their decision. There are numerous ways to do this, some of which might include:

- ☆ Having a ring ceremony where we place a "promise" ring on our child's wedding finger to commemorate his or her commitment to premarital abstinence (churches often host such ceremonies).

- ☆ Inviting family and friends over to the house for a special dinner, at which time our kids can explain the commitment they have made and why they have made it.

- ☆ Prompting our kids to write a letter to their future spouse explaining their commitment to wait for him or her. We can then frame and display the letter as a memorial of their decision—and wouldn't that framed letter make an amazing wedding gift for our kids to give to their future mates someday?

Do any of these ideas appeal to you and your child? Do you have another idea? However we decide to celebrate, the key is that we do, in fact, celebrate our child's decision to commit to premarital abstinence.

I have just one note of caution—we must make sure we don't prompt a premature celebration *before* our kids have sincerely arrived at a personal decision to remain abstinent. As reiterated throughout this book, the choice is ultimately theirs, not ours.

ADDITIONAL STEPS

Here are more practical tips we can give our kids in an effort to see their commitment to premarital abstinence stand the test of time.

1. Hang around like-minded people.

If our kids want to keep their commitment to abstinence going strong, they should avoid making friends with people whose lifestyles contradict their commitment. When we're in pursuit of sexual purity, we don't have any business hanging around with sexually active people or friends who entertain themselves with sexually graphic media. There's an old saying, "You are what you eat." Likewise, we become what we are surrounded by. Case in point, our kids should surround themselves with peers who point them in the right direction, not peers who pull them away from their goals.

And for Pete's sake, they shouldn't date someone who doesn't have their same commitment to sexual purity! That's like trying to run a marathon with a sumo wrestler riding on their back. (Feel free to pause a moment to reflect on that mental image.)

2. Be smart.

One day while sitting in a college algebra class, a guy sat down next to me and expressed how very nervous he was about taking the test that was soon to be distributed. He went on and on about how badly he wanted to pass and how he desired to get a really good grade in the course. Ironically, when I asked him how long he studied for the test he said, "I didn't."

Throughout this book, we've gone over lots of principles and practices that will help our kids succeed in their quest to be abstinent, but they must *apply* these principles in order for them to work. They can't expect to coast through their single years without compromising their commitment to abstinence unless they are willing to follow through with the various steps and strategies as depicted in this book (and other quality materials relating to abstinence).

They say elephants never forget a thing, but since we are not elephants, we have to review and remind ourselves of things from time to time. For this reason, you will want to go through this study with your child again in the future, along with any other books that help remind him why he chose abstinence in the first place. As previously stated, however, they must apply what they learn if it's going to do any good.

3. Pray.

Pray with your child for his or her future mate on a regular basis. Also, encourage your teenager to continually pray about his or her commitment to abstinence. In the same way that gasoline powers a vehicle, prayer fuels our spiritual convictions and commitments. Remind your child that the best way to overcome carnal lusts is to depend on the Holy Spirit. Our dependence is renewed when we pray.

THE MOST ESSENTIAL POINT

Unless the Lord builds a house, the work of the builders is wasted. Unless the Lord protects a city, guarding it with sentries will do no good (Psalm 127:1 NLT).

Mom or Dad, are your children born-again? Do you know what I mean by that? I'm asking if your children have repented of their sins, cried out to Christ as their Savior, and bowed a knee to Christ as the Lord of their life.

Too many times we operate with a false spiritual assurance based on the fact that we understand that Jesus died for our sins. In reality, relating to Christ as our Savior is just *part* of the salvation process, not the culmination.

If you confess with your mouth that Jesus is Lord and believe in your heart that God raised Him from the dead [Savior], you will be saved (Romans 10:9 NLT).

Somewhere in our country's spiritual history, we started separating Savior and Lord, as if we could accept Christ as our Savior but postpone (or forego) making Him the Master (Lord) of our lives. This is my testimony. I thought that because I had walked down to an altar and repeated a prayer for salvation, as prompted by a minister, I was saved. What I didn't realize at the time was that *salvation was not just about accepting Christ's sacrifice on my behalf, but about offering my life as a living sacrifice on His behalf!*

As I stood at that altar, I wanted the assurance of going to Heaven, but I had no intention of relinquishing the proverbial throne of my heart over to God. I walked back to my sanctuary chair with a pamphlet in hand that assured me that I was saved, but in my heart, I was as self-willed as I had always been. It wasn't until a series of hardships humbled me later in life that I came to the end of myself and made the decision to follow Christ. I am confident that I became born-again in that moment—all alone in my bedroom with my Bible, tear-stained cheeks, and a heartfelt prayer—not when I went up to the altar and repeated a prayer years prior. Emotions were involved in my born-again experience, but it was the drastic, permanent change in my inner desires and motives that showed me that the transformation was more than emotional; *it was a miraculous spiritual conversion.*

The Book of Acts contains the biblical account of the launch of the New Testament Church. Throughout the book, Christ is referred to as Savior *two* times, but as Lord (the Greek word is *kurious*), 92 times! Case in point, Christ never intended to serve as our Savior without being revered as our Lord. Furthermore, there is no scriptural basis for salvation outside of the Lordship of Christ in our lives.

Instead of facing the reality that their child is on his way to hell, some parents will cling to false hopes so they can sleep at night.[1]

Am I saying that we have to have our lives totally in order before we can come to Christ? Absolutely not! And I am also not saying that the moment we become born-again we no longer act selfish or sinful at times. What I *am* saying is that, in addition to desiring for Christ to save us, there must be authentic repentance and a willingness to yield to His Lordship. Parents, it's our responsibility to make sure our kids are aware of this.

For more information on how to lead your child to salvation, I strongly recommend Ray Comfort's book, *How to Bring Your Children to Christ and Keep Them There*.[2]

GOOD NEWS FOR PARENTS

When our kids experience authentic salvation based on the Gospel of repentance as communicated by Jesus Christ (see Luke 13:3), something wonderful happens! The Holy Spirit comes to dwell in them and gives them new desires and motivations (see 2 Cor. 5:17). One of these desires includes a hunger for sexual purity. This internal motivation resonating from the Spirit of God inside our children supersedes any efforts that you or I could possibly achieve by means of communication or sex education. While these are all beneficial and necessary, Christ's Lordship in our kids' lives is the ultimate motivator for right living. When our kids are yielded to the leadership of the Holy Spirit, abstinence becomes a natural byproduct.

Therefore, if anyone is in Christ, he is a new creation; old things have passed away; behold, all things have become new (2 Corinthians 5:17).

The wisdom of Psalm 127:1 rings true and bears repeating: "Unless the Lord builds a house, the work of the builders is wasted. Unless the Lord protects a city, guarding it with sentries will do no good" (NLT). In other words, unless the Lordship of Christ is the foundation of our kids' morality, we're not going to get very far with all of our behavior modification efforts.

Parents, our ultimate goal should be to lead our children to an understanding of the *unaltered* Gospel message of Christ so that the Spirit might reveal to them the need for repentance, a Savior, and Christ's Lordship. (I have included a quiz in the Appendix of this book that is designed to convey the message of salvation to young people.) After all, what good is it for our children to marry as virgins, live the all-American dream, and then face their Creator without the assurance of Christ's eternal saving power?

A GLIMPSE OF THE FUTURE

Can you believe that we have already arrived at the end of our study? I'd like to conclude by giving you one last exercise. You will want to read the following description out loud to your child and then discuss the all-important question posed at the end:

You sit up in bed after a somewhat restless night of sleep and already the butterflies fill your stomach. Today is one of the most important days of your entire life—your wedding day! In a matter of hours, you will stand in front of your parents, family, friends, and almighty God and make a lifelong commitment to honor and cherish the love of your life. From this moment on, you will share every day with your special soul mate until the two of you have no more days left to share.

Your mind quickly jogs back to the many memories you have already made with your fiancé—times you've laughed so hard you couldn't breathe and moments you felt such love and adoration it took your breath away. As wonderful as the memories are, excitement fills your soul to think that there are countless memories that have yet to be made!

It's time to get out of bed and get ready, but your heart is so overwhelmed with gratitude that you simply have to talk to God first. In the stillness of the moment, you begin to pray.

"Lord, I have dreamed of this day for many years, and now you have fulfilled my desire. How can I thank you for bringing me such a wonderful spouse? I am honored that you lovingly set apart such a wonderful person for me. I am both humbled and amazed at your ability to not only answer my prayers, but to pour out blessings that far exceed my expectations. May my marriage be a continual delight in your sight, Lord. May I love my precious spouse with the same devotion and passion that you have always loved me."

Now ask yourself, *was it worth the wait?*

May God guide you continually and bless your family for generations to come as you labor to inspire sexual purity and spiritual passion in your child!

Questions for Thought

1. Do you have any ideas about how you might celebrate your child's commitment to premarital abstinence?

2. Have you been praying with your child for his or her future mate? Why or why not?

3. Do you relate to Christ as your Savior or as your Savior and Lord? Why is this important?

4. Has your child accepted Christ as the Savior and Lord of his life? Do you feel confident that you could explain salvation to him with biblical accuracy? If not, how might you become equipped?

5. What is the most valuable thing you have learned during this study? What do you plan to do as a result?

APPENDIX
QUIZ: Am I a Good Person?

Put a check next to your answers.

1. Do you think you're a good person?

❏ *Yes* ❏ *No*

Let me guess, you checked yes. After all, you've never killed anyone, and you try to do good things when you have the opportunity, right? I'm sure, compared to the average "Joe," you truly are an outstanding citizen.

2. Are you familiar with the Ten Commandments?

❏ *Yes* ❏ *No*

While we tend to compare ourselves to other people (like criminals for example) in order to feel good about the kind of person we are,

God gave us the Ten Commandments as the standard or "measuring stick" that we could use to evaluate our personal goodness. Let's look at three of the commandments and see how we measure up.

3. **Have you ever lied?**

❏ *Yes*   ❏ *No*

Of course you have—we have all broken this commandment. As a matter of fact, if you said no, you're lying! And what do we call people who lie? Yep, we call them *liars* (or *no-good, rotten, "stinkin" liars* if it's someone who lied to us personally).

4. **Have you ever disobeyed your parents?**

❏ *Yes*   ❏ *No*

If I was a gambler, I'd bet the farm that you have deliberately disobeyed your parents on more than one occasion. (I don't own a farm, but you get the point.) I wasn't exactly a perfect angel growing up myself, so I am just as guilty of breaking this commandment as you are. Friend, you and I have been rebellious, haven't we?

5. **Have you ever stolen anything?**

❏ *Yes*   ❏ *No*

Okay, maybe you haven't robbed a bank at gunpoint, but have you ever taken something that didn't belong to you? I remember taking money out of a girl's purse in the locker room in junior high. Pathetic, I know. And what do we call people who steal? Not stealers—*thieves*.

6. **Do you still think you're a good person?**

❏ *Yes*   ❏ *Heck No!*

We've looked at just three of the Ten Commandments, and already you and I have proven to be lying, thieving, rebellious people! To make matters worse, the Bible says that God is going to judge us by those Ten Commandments. So what's the verdict on you?

7. **If God judged you by His Ten Commandments, do you think you would be found innocent or guilty?**

   ❏ *Umm…innocent*   ❏ *Guilty*

If you said innocent, I just have one thing to say—"Denial, party of one, your table is now available!" You have broken God's laws just like I have, and we are guilty. To deny that we are guilty of breaking God's laws is illogical. Our own conscience tells us we're guilty every time we do something we know is wrong, doesn't it?

8. **What do you plan to do about your guilt?**

   ❏ *Try to make up for it by doing good things, like going to church and giving money to the poor.*

   ❏ *Hope I discover a fountain of immortality so I never have to die and stand before God to give account for my actions.*

   ❏ *Nothing; there's nothing I can do about it.*

If you said you plan to do good things to make up for your guilt, I have some bad news for you—God will not accept that. Think about it, would a good judge let a man guilty of murder go free because he had volunteered at a food pantry a few times? I know you've never murdered anyone, but Jesus said that if we've ever hated anyone, we have committed murder in our hearts (ouch!). The truth is, there's really nothing we can do to erase our guilt. If we try to quit sinning, we will only get frustrated because we can't stop; besides, it wouldn't change the fact that we have sinned in the past.

9. **What do you think will happen if you stand before God** guilty of breaking the Ten Commandments?

   ❏ *He'll understand I meant well and let me into Heaven anyway.*

   ❏ I'll go to hell.

If Heaven is a perfect place like the Bible describes, yet God is willing to simply wink at our sin and let liars, thieves, and rebellious people like us in, Heaven won't be perfect for long, will it? The Bible is clear that all sinners are separated from God relationally and, therefore, upon dying, go to the place where His presence cannot be found—hell.

10. Does that concern you?

❏ *Not really*   ❏ *YES!*

Right now, while you're young and healthy, it may be easy to say that you're not worried about where you will go when you die, but what do you think it would be like to be on your death bed, knowing that you are going to face eternity and God any minute? Of course it's a terrifying thought to think that we could end up in hell, separated from God forever...and ever... and ever... and ever... OK, my brain hurts!

11. Is God a big fat "meanie"?

❏ *It kinda seems that way!*   ❏ *No*

If God knew good and well that you and I couldn't keep the Ten Commandments perfectly and that we would just end up in hell, why did He give us those blasted commandments in the first place? Allow me to answer this important question. One reason God gave us the Ten Commandments is so that we would realize that we *can't* keep them; thus, we would recognize our need for a Savior (i.e. Jesus Christ). You see, man is intrinsically proud and self-reliant, but God's Commandments act as a mirror and show us how "ugly" we really are. It's only when we see our true reflection in the mirror of God's law that we come to understand reality, which is that we are desperate for God's intervention and help!

12. Do you know what God did so that you don't have to be punished for your sins?

❏ *He told mankind that we could all just make up what we think is the way to Heaven and that He would honor all of our creative ideas.*

❏ *He sent His Son, Jesus Christ, to take the punishment that we deserve.*

While there are many religions in the earth, only one actually deals with the issue at hand—man's broken relationship with God as a result of our sin. Every world religion involves earning one's right standing (righteousness) with God through good works, except one: *Christianity.* Romans 1:8 says, *"For the wages* [earned consequences] of sin is death [physical and eternal separation from God], *but the free gift of God is eternal life through Christ Jesus,"* (NLT). In other words, the punishment and payment for our sins is impossible for any of us to pay, so God lovingly paid it for us by sending His Son, Jesus Christ, to be punished in our place (by death on the cross). Simply put, humanity has one huge problem—sin—and God gave one mandatory solution—Jesus Christ. It really is that simple!

13. So how do I go about getting forgiven?

❏ *Just say some little prayer about inviting Jesus into your heart and then you will never have to think about all that spiritual stuff anymore; you're safe from hell.*

❏ *Read your Bible all day, every day and never sin again and then Jesus will accept you.*

❏ *Repent for your sins and start a new life with Jesus as your Lord and Savior.*

We don't get saved by repeating some prayer that we don't really mean and then living the same old self-centered life we always have. We also don't get saved by being "good religious folk" who memorize the Bible and try to be perfect. Salvation is relational, meaning that it occurs not by *what we do,* but by *whom we choose* to love and trust. We:

☆ **Acknowledge our sin** instead of making excuses and trying to justify our actions.

☆ **Repent for our sinful heart**, which means we turn away from a life of self-centeredness and self-reliance apart from God and rely on Him instead.

☆ **Accept Christ's sacrifice on our behalf** by acknowledging that we cannot earn salvation but must receive it based on what Christ already did for us on the cross.

☆ **Commit to live with Christ as our Lord** out of a heart of gratitude for the fact that He died for us.

14. Is there a formal prayer that I need to pray?

❏ *Yes, you must pray certain words while seated in a certain position in a certain place on a certain day of the week for a certain amount of time.*

❏ *Nope!*

Just pray from your heart. The Bible says that, when you confess and turn from your sins and put your trust in Christ, the Holy Spirit will literally come and dwell in you and lead you for the rest of your life to the degree that you yield to His leadership. How cool is that?

15. Then will I be allowed into Heaven when I die?

❏ *Maybe; maybe not.*

❏ *Yes!*

If Christ is our Lord and Savior, we are welcomed into Heaven, into God's awesome presence, when we die, because God no longer sees us as sinners. He sees us as His beloved children! Our past sins are forgiven and any sins that we commit in the future are covered under the blood of Jesus.

So why don't we just keep on sinning? Well that's just it—once we're saved, we don't like to sin. Sure, sin is still tempting, but the

Holy Spirit gives us a strong desire to resist sin and live for God. In those times of weakness when we *do* give in to sin, we feel horrible—not because we fear that God is going to reject us or give up on us (remember, we're God's children now!), but because we love our Heavenly Father and want to please Him.

So what do you think? Do you need to set this book down and have a little "heart-to-heart" with God? I tell you what, having that talk with God was the best thing I ever did—not because life has been easy since then, but because I now know what I'm living for.

Endnotes

CHAPTER ONE: FORCING
WHAT'S WRONG WITH FORCING ABSTINENCE?

1. "Teens and Sex: Stop Worrying, Start Talking," *Better Homes and Gardens,* September 8, 2007, http://www.bhg.com/health-family/parenting-skills (accessed 22 Oct 2008).

2. The Henry J. Kaiser Family Foundation, "U.S. Teen Sexual Activity" (Menlo Park, CA: January 2005), 1-2; http://www.kff.org/youthhivstds/upload/U-S-Teen-Sexual-Activity-Fact-Sheet.pdf (accessed 22 Oct 2008).

3. Ray Comfort, *How to Bring Your Children to Christ and Keep Them There: Avoiding the Tragedy of False Conversion* (OK: Genesis Publishing Group, 2005).

4. Kathleen Stassen Berger, *The Developing Person Through the Lifespan*, 7th ed. (New York: Worth Publishers, 2008), 422.

5. The Henry J. Kaiser Family Foundation, "U.S. Teen Sexual Activity," 1-2.

6. Berger, 421.

7. John Townsend, *Boundaries With Teens: When to Say Yes, How to Say No* (Grand Rapids, MI: Zondervan, 2006).

8. The Henry J. Kaiser Family Foundation, "Virginity and the First Time" (Menlo Park, CA: October 2003), 4; http://www.kff.org/entpartnerships/upload/Virginity-and-the-First-Time-Summary-of-Findings.pdf (accessed 22 Oct 2008).

Chapter Two: Warning
I've Warned My Child—Isn't That Enough?

1. Katie Couric, "Nearly 3 in 10 young teens sexually active: NBC News, People Magazine Commission Landmark Poll," *The 411: Teens and Sex: A Katie Couric Special*, January 31, 2005, http://www.msnbc.msn.com/id/6872269/ (accessed 22 Oct 2008).

2. The Henry J. Kaiser Family Foundation, "Virginity and the First Time" (Menlo Park, CA: October 2003), 4; http://www.kff.org/entpartnerships/upload/Virginity-and-the-First-Time-Summary-of-Findings.pdf (accessed 22 Oct 2008).

3. Couric.

4. Kathleen Stassen Berger, *The Developing Person Through the Lifespan*, 7th ed. (New York: Worth Publishers, 2008), 419.

5. Check out these excellent resources for biblical literacy and apologetics:

- Answers In Genesis (www.answersingenesis.org);
- The Truth Project (www.thetruthproject.org);
- The Way of the Master (www.wayofthemaster.com);
- Ergun Mehmet Caner, *When Worldviews Collide: Christians Confronting Culture* (Nashville, TN: LifeWay Press, 2005), www.lifeway.com; and
- Peter D. Kreeft and Ronald Tacelli, *Handbook of Christian Apologetics* (Downers Grove, IL: InterVarsity Press, 1994), www.ivpress.com.

CHAPTER THREE: INSTILLING
EFFECTIVE ABSTINENCE APPROACH

1. Bill Albert, *With One Voice: America's Adults and Teens Sound Off About Teen Pregnancy* (Washington DC: National Campaign to Prevent Teen Pregnancy, 2004), 4, www.thenationalcampaign.org/national-data/pdf/WOV2004.pdf (accessed 22 Oct 2008).

2. Linda Lyons, "Teens' Marriage Views Reflect Changing Norms," *The Gallup Organization* (November 18, 2003).

3. Mary Beth Marklein, "Spiritual students mostly lean right," *USA Today* (July 28, 2004).

CHAPTER FOUR: DELEGATING
ISN'T IT THE CHURCH'S RESPONSIBILITY?

1. Diane E. Papalia, Sally Wendkos Olds, and Ruth Duskin Feldman, *A Child's Developing Word, Infancy Through Adolescence,* 11th ed. (New York: McGraw-Hill Higher Education, 2008), 482.

2. Kathleen Stassen Berger, *The Developing Person Through the Lifespan,* 7th ed. (New York: Worth Publishers, 2008), 430.

Chapter Five: Home Life
What Affects a Child's Sexuality?

1. John Eldredge, *Wild at Heart: Discovering the Secret of a Man's Soul* (Nashville, TN: Thomas Nelson, 2001); and John Eldredge and Staci Elderedge, *Captivating: Unveiling the Mystery of a Woman's Soul* (Nashville, TN: Thomas Nelson, 2007).

2. Diane E. Papalia, Sally Wendkos Olds, and Ruth Duskin Feldman, *A Child's Developing Word, Infancy Through Adolescence,* 11th ed. (New York: McGraw-Hill Higher Education, 2008), 476.

3. Bill Albert, *With One Voice: America's Adults and Teens Sound Off About Teen Pregnancy* (Washington DC: National Campaign to Prevent Teen Pregnancy, 2004), 6, www.thenationalcampaign.org/national-data/pdf/WOV2004.pdf (accessed 22 Oct 2008).

4. Papalia, Olds, and Feldman, 476.

5. Joseph Nicolosi, PhD, *Reparative Therapy of Male Homosexuality: a New Clinical Approach* (Northvale, NJ: Jason Arson Inc., 1991).

6. Ibid.

7. Kathleen Stassen Berger, *The Developing Person Through the Lifespan,* 7th ed. (New York: Worth Publishers, 2008), 431.

8. Ibid., 436.

9. Ibid., 431.

10. National Coalition for the Protection of Families and Children, "Current Statistics," http://www.puremorality.org/NCPCFstats.htm (accessed 18 Sept 2008).

11. Papalia, Olds, and Feldman, 478.

12. National Coalition for the Protection of Families and Children, "Current Statistics."

CHAPTER SIX: TIMING
HOW OLD FOR SEX TALK?

1. Diane E. Papalia, Sally Wendkos Olds, and Ruth Duskin Feldman, *A Child's Developing Word, Infancy Through Adolescence*, 11th ed. (New York: McGraw-Hill Higher Education, 2008), 476.

2. Kathleen Stassen Berger, *The Developing Person Through the Lifespan*, 7th ed. (New York: Worth Publishers, 2008), 431.

3. Papalia, Olds, and Feldman, 475.

4. The National Campaign to Prevent Teen Pregnancy, "Parents and Teen Pregnancy: What Surveys Show," September 2003, www.thenationalcampaign.org/national-data/pdf/Parentspollingfactoids2004.pdf (accessed 23 Oct 2008).

5. Berger, 431.

6. Ibid., 436.

CHAPTER SEVEN: SACRED
WHAT'S SO SACRED ABOUT SEX?

1. Cheryl Wetzstein. "Sexually transmitted infection rates soar among youth," *The Washington Times*, March 17, 2004.

2. Maggie Fox. "Sex Map Shows Chain of Almost 300 High School Lovers," *Reuters*, January 24, 2005.

3. Robert Rector, Kirk Johnson, and Lauren Noyes. "Sexually Active Teenagers Are More Likely to Be Depressed and to Attempt Suicide," *The Heritage Foundation*, June 3, 2003.

4. Ibid.

5. Manda Aufochs Gillespie, "STDs and Condoms: Are You Really Safe?" *The F News Magazine*, August 8, 2008, http://www.fnewsmagazine.com/2005-feb/current/pages/5.shtml (accessed 23 Oct 2008).

6. Bill Albert, *With One Voice: America's Adults and Teens Sound Off About Teen Pregnancy* (Washington DC: National Campaign to Prevent Teen Pregnancy, 2004), 5, www.thenationalcampaign.org/national-data/pdf/WOV2004.pdf (accessed 22 Oct 2008).

7. Kathleen Stassen Berger, *The Developing Person Through the Lifespan*, 7th ed. (New York: Worth Publishers, 2008), 594.

CHAPTER EIGHT: SIN
WHY IS PREMARITAL SEX A SIN?

1. Kathleen Stassen Berger, *The Developing Person Through the Lifespan*, 7th ed. (New York: Worth Publishers, 2008), 508.

2. The Henry J. Kaiser Family Foundation, "Virginity and the First Time" (Menlo Park, CA: October 2003), Fig. 3; http://www.kff.org/entpartnerships/upload/Virginity-and-the-First-Time-Summary-of-Findings.pdf (accessed 22 Oct 2008).

3. Joyce Howard Price, "Teens want to wait for sex," *The Washington Times*, December 2003.

4. Sue Johanson, "Sex Talk With Sue Johanson," *Sex Talk*, August 8, 2007, http://www.talksexwithsue.com/condoms.html (accessed 23 Oct 2008).

5. Robert Rector, Kirk Johnson, and Lauren Noyes, "Sexually Active Teenagers Are More Likely to Be Depressed and to Attempt Suicide," *The Heritage Foundation*, June 3, 2003.

6. Bridget E. Maher, "Abstinence Until Marriage: The Best Message for Teens," *Family Research Council*, September 7, 2004.

CHAPTER NINE: VIRGINITY
HOW TO CONVEY THE VALUE OF VIRGINITY

1. Lauren F. Winner, "Sex in the Body of Christ," *Christianity Today*, May 2005, http://www.puremorality.org/NCPCFstats.htm (accessed 23 Oct 2008).

2. Kathleen Stassen Berger, *The Developing Person Through the Lifespan*, 7th ed. (New York: Worth Publishers, 2008), 454.

3. Ibid.

CHAPTER TEN: FOREPLAY
HOW FAR IS TOO FAR?

1. Sharon Jayson, "Technical Virginity becomes part of teens' equation," *USA Today*, October 19, 2005.

2. Ed Wheat MD and Gayle Wheat, *Intended for Pleasure: Sex Technique and Sexual Fulfillment in Christian Marriage* (Grand Rapids, MI: Fleming H. Revell, 1976), 74.

3. Sharon Jayson, "Survey: Many teenagers have oral sex," *USA Today*, September 9, 2005.

4. Caroline Stanley, "Oral Sex: A Dangerous Teen Trend," *Ladies' Home Journal*, 2004.

CHAPTER ELEVEN: DATING
WHAT ABOUT DATING?

1. Lauren F. Winner, "Sex in the Body of Christ," *Christianity Today*, May 2005.

2. Shannon Ethridge, "Mama, don't let your babies grow up to be sexually ignorant," *Enrichment Journal*, 2005.

3. Kathleen Stassen Berger, *The Developing Person Through the Lifespan*, 7th ed. (New York: Worth Publishers, 2008), 380.

4. Ibid., 381.

5. Ibid.

6. "Teens and Sex: Stop Worrying, Start Talking," *Better Homes and Gardens*, September 8, 2007, www.bhg.com/health-family/parenting-skills (accessed 22 Oct 2008).

7. "Current Statistics," *National Coalition for the Protection of Children and Families*, http://www.puremorality.org/NCPCFstats.htm (accessed 23 Oct 2008).

CHAPTER TWELVE: OBJECTIONS
RESPONDING TO OBJECTIONS AND MYTHS ABOUT ABSTINENCE

1. For additional objections, rebuttals, questions, and answers, log on to www.InspiredAbstinence.com.

2. The Henry J. Kaiser Family Foundation, "Virginity and the First Time" (Menlo Park, CA: October 2003), Fig. 6; http://www.kff.org/entpartnerships/upload/Virginity-and-the-First-Time-Summary-of-Findings.pdf (accessed 22 Oct 2008).

3. Ibid, Fig. 1.

4. Ed Wheat MD and Gayle Wheat, *Intended for Pleasure: Sex Technique and Sexual Fulfillment in Christian Marriage* (Grand Rapids, MI: Fleming H. Revell, 1976), 74.

5. "America's Families and Living Arrangements: 2003," *U.S. Department of Commerce, U.S. Census Bureau*, November 2004.

6. Matthew D. Bramlett PhD and William D. Mosher PhD, "First Marriage Dissolution, Divorce, and Remarriage: United States," Advance Data No. 232 (Hyattsville, MD:

Centers for Disease Control and Prevention, May 31, 2001), 1-2, http://www.cdc.gov/nchs/data/ad/ad323.pdf (accessed 24 Oct 2008).

7. "Cohabitation: A Recipe for Martial Ruin," *A Zenit Daily Dispatch*, October 1, 2005.

8. "Divorce May Be the Cost of Living Together First," *New York Times*, January 30, 2008.

9. "Cohabitation: A Recipe for Martial Ruin."

10. Ibid.

11. Ibid.

12. Ibid.

CHAPTER THIRTEEN: MARRIAGE
PREPARING A CHILD TO CHOOSE THE RIGHT MATE

1. Kathleen Stassen Berger, *The Developing Person Through the Lifespan*, 7th ed. (New York: Worth Publishers, 2008), 432.

2. Peter Lord, *Hearing God* (Grand Rapids, MI: Baker Books).

3. Berger, 595.

4. Diane E. Papalia, Sally Wendkos Olds, and Ruth Duskin Feldman, *A Child's Developing Word, Infancy Through Adolescence*, 11th ed. (New York: McGraw-Hill Higher Education, 2008), 48.

CHAPTER FOURTEEN: RENEWAL
NO LONGER A VIRGIN?

1. Diane E. Papalia, Sally Wendkos Olds, and Ruth Duskin Feldman, *A Child's Developing Word, Infancy Through Adolescence*, 11th ed. (New York: McGraw-Hill Higher Education, 2008), 480.

2. Ibid., 475.

3. Ibid., 477.

4. Ibid., 478.

5. Ibid., 482.

CHAPTER FIFTEEN: LONG TERM SUCCESS
ENCOURAGING ABSTINENCE COMMITMENT

1. Ray Comfort, *How to Bring Your Children to Christ and Keep Them There: Avoiding the Tragedy of False Conversion* (OK: Genesis Publishing Group, 2005).

2. Ibid.

About the Author

Motivated by a passion for the preservation of family values, Laura B. Gallier has spent the last decade as a youth minister and advisor to teens and parents. She and her husband, Patrick, live in Cypress, Texas, and maintain an adventurous home life that consists of three children, two hermit crabs, a dog, and one temperamental fish.

As the founder of Inspiring Abstinence, Laura currently seeks opportunities to partner with community leaders to launch effective abstinence campaigns in schools, churches, and other public venues.

Inspiring Abstinence is a faith-based endeavor that seeks to:

- Equip parents to inspire sexual purity in their kids, and

- Empower teens to make solid decisions concerning sex and their future.

- By combining research, logic, and experience, and by building on a biblical foundation, the message of Inspiring Abstinence is both timely and effective.

REQUEST FOR PERSONAL APPEARANCE:

Interested in launching an Inspiring Abstinence campaign in your community? Laura is willing to take her message on the road!

To contact Laura Gallier visit:

www.inspiringabstinence.com

or

write info@inspiringabstinence.com

Additional copies of this book and other
book titles from DESTINY IMAGE are
available at your local bookstore.

Call toll-free: 1-800-722-6774.

Send a request for a catalog to:

Destiny Image® Publishers, Inc.

P.O. Box 310
Shippensburg, PA·17257-0310

*"Speaking to the Purposes of God for this
Generation and for the Generations to Come."*

**For a complete list of our titles,
visit us at www.destinyimage.com.**